in
ogy

11

Editorial Committee

Mary Grey
Lisa Isherwood
Janet Wootton

Sheffield Academic Press
A Continuum imprint

Introducing Feminist Perspectives on Pastoral Theology

Zoë Bennett Moore

Copyright © 2002 Sheffield Academic Press
A Continuum imprint

Published by Sheffield Academic Press Ltd
The Tower Building, 11 York Road, London SE1 7NX
370 Lexington Avenue, New York NY 10017-6550

www.continuumbooks.com

British Library Cataloguing-in-Publication Data

A catalogue record for this book is available from the British Library

Typeset by Sheffield Academic Press
Printed on acid-free paper in Great Britain by MPG Books Ltd, Bodmin, Cornwall

ISBN 0-8264-6261-8

Table of Contents

Introduction

The proclamation that God is love is at the heart of Christian belief, and the practice of love is at the heart of Christianity. 'God is love, and those who abide in love abide in God and God abides in them... We love because he first loved us. Those who say, "I love God", and hate their brothers or sisters, are liars...' (1 Jn 4.16, 19-20). This insight about the nature of God, of human community and of the connections between them is central to the discipline and practice of pastoral theology.

Much debate will be found among pastoral and practical theologians concerning the precise meanings and value of the various terms such as pastoral theology, practical theology or pastoral studies.[1] Some of the issues turn around different usage in different contexts, particularly differences between British, European and North American usage, while other issues turn around more serious questions about the identity of the discipline (Miller-McLemore 1998). In this book I take a wide definition of pastoral theology as critical reflection on the practices of the Christian community. This includes not only the community's practices of direct pastoral care (Miller-McLemore 1999: 91), but also 'the horizons of value embodied in all intentional practices of faith' (Graham 1996: 209) including, for example, ethics, worship and education (Graham 1999b).

I am drawn to both terms—*pastoral* and *theology*. The word *pastoral*, while problematic from a feminist perspective in its uncritical association with shepherding and in particular with sheep, as I shall explore in Chapter 1, is helpful in holding before us an image of caring which is both imaginatively suggestive and centrally focused on the practices of loving concern. The word *theology* reminds us that our concern is with God. Pastoral theology is a theologically disclosive discipline (Graham 1996; Elford 1999).

---

1. Ballard and Pritchard 1996; Graham 1996; Miller-McLemore 1999: 90; Carr 1997 (Woodward and Pattison 2000).

It is perfectly possible to examine practices of care from the perspectives of sociology or of psychology, for example, without bringing in the dimension of the divine at all, let alone the resources of the Christian tradition. Indeed there are those who would claim that much of what passes for pastoral theology has done just this (Oden 1984). Pastoral theology, however, as a branch of Christian theology (Hiltner 1958) must seek to engage *'omnia sub ratione dei'*—'all things... in terms of God...because they are relative to him as their origin and end' (Aquinas, *Summa Theologiae* 1a.1, 7). It must seek to ask the questions posed *by* faith and the gospel in relation to the practices of communities of faith, and the questions put *to* faith and the gospel arising from the diverse life of communities of faith in the world. Pastoral theology's particular focus is the study of the 'living human document' (a term first used by Anton Boisen to indicate the importance of the interpretation of people and life situations not just of written texts) or the 'living human web' (Miller-McLemore 1996). Its central method is one of critical correlation—bringing the questions and the answers raised and offered by theology and by secular disciplines, by faith and the world, into mutual dialogue and critique.

A Feminist Perspective on Pastoral Theology

This book has its origins in an MA module which I teach, Feminist Perspectives on Pastoral Theology. This module is part of a taught MA in Pastoral Theology, which is offered by the Cambridge Theological Federation and validated by Anglia Polytechnic University. Feminist Perspectives is taught each year to a group of eight to fourteen students—some women, some men; some lay, some ordained; of varying ages and backgrounds—most of whom are new to feminist theology.

The key aim of the module is to engage the experiences of women in the church—represented both by the stories of participants and by wider exposure to women's experience through reading, listening and observing—into a dialogue that draws in both feminist perspectives and theological perspectives. We pay attention to the traditions of the church and Christian theology, and seek out the ways in which both women's experience and theoretical feminist perspectives raise problems for church practice and for theology. In particular we ask what it means for women to name themselves as made in the image of God. Students are asked to present a project based on a feminist and theological critique of an issue related to the theme of 'the body'. Both the teaching throughout the module and the form of the assessment involve dialogical and experiential learning, and seek to maximize creative and affective engagement (Bennett Moore 2002a).

So for a feminist perspective the key words *pastoral* and *theology* are again important. *Pastoral* indicates the rootedness in experience that is central to feminist theological method, and points towards those areas of love and care, of relationality and flourishing, which are both significant and problematic for women. As for *theology*, it is of the utmost importance to a feminist critique that the 'God dimension' is not overlooked. As I will argue, there is an intimate connection between the community's beliefs about and images for God and the values given by that community to human beings and to human practices.

Elaine Graham has recently identified three priorities for British feminist practical theology: the 'dialogue with the discipline as a whole, the dialogue across ethnic and racial boundaries, and dialogue with "secular" feminists' (1998: 149). To these I would add a fourth: the dialogue between feminist pastoral theology and traditions of Christian belief and of Christian ministry. Given that I work in the context of teaching pastoral theology to those in or preparing for ministry in various branches of the Christian church, my concern is rooted in my personal practice of pastoral ministry (I consider teaching to be such a pastoral practice). In a North American context Bonnie Miller-McLemore and Brita Gill-Austern have identified theological education as a key locus of pastoral theology and 'theological understandings of human nature and salvation' as a key area to which feminist pastoral theology must contribute (Miller-McLemore and Gill-Austern 1999: 14; Gill-Austern 1999). They want to see 'more attention to educative models—how to build healing and transforming communities' (1999: 18). The first essay in this important recently published volume indicates, as a future pointer, the need to attend to the 'profoundly ambivalent relationship between the discipline and the institutional church' (Greider, Johnson and Leslie 1999: 48). It is within this 'profoundly ambivalent relationship' that I find myself situated. I hope that this book may be a contribution from that specific place, where the issues of theological education, of theological understandings of God, human nature and salvation, and the issues of the 'building of healing and transformative communities' in the context of church-related ministry, are addressed in all their pain and ambiguity.

The Shape of this Book

In Chapter 1 I ask the question, 'Who needs a feminist perspective?' and, in answering, trace some of the history of recent work in feminist pastoral theology, examine methodological issues concerning both understanding and practice, and finally look at the meaning of 'feminist' in this context. Three principles guide the shape of what follows. The first is that *it is appropriate for feminist pastoral theology to start from life experience and to move to a theorizing of that experience, and to a critique of existing theory.* Chapter 2 will therefore tackle a key issue in women's life experience—violence. To foreground the issue of violence serves not only to bring vividly into focus a deeply serious area involving women's lives and pastoral care, it also provides a standpoint from which to ask critical questions concerning society and the church, and to analyse their undergirding values and theology. A feminist is someone who acknowledges the patriarchal nature of the structures of society (including the church) and who seeks to change them. An acknowledgment of the concrete forms violence takes, and an analysis of the hidden violence implicit in the very nature of patriarchal structures, are essential aspects of the feminist project.

The second principle is that *feminist pastoral theology will involve a critique of existing Christian beliefs and doctrines.* Hence Chapters 3 to 5 visit traditional Christian theological sources and beliefs with an awareness of the acute seriousness of the problems raised in Chapter 2. It has too often been assumed either that the tradition is irredeemably patriarchal and damaging, or that it is in itself life-giving but has been misinterpreted and misused. Both of these assumptions are naive. A more sophisticated examination and hermeneutic is required. Chapter 3 looks at the Bible, asking questions of its use—in pastoral care, in liturgy, in proclamation—and at questions of abuse: is the Bible abused? Is it abusive? The Bible is centrally important for Christian feminist pastoral theology, given both its key historical and contemporary role in the liberation and in the oppression of women, and also its comparatively long history of attention from feminist scholars. Chapters 4 and 5 are concerned with the doctrine of *imago dei*. It is impossible to disentangle the images we have of God from the way we think of ourselves as made in God's image. These chapters explore the problems of ideology and of language thus raised, and examine the significance for feminist pastoral theology of our doctrine of God, our Christology and our beliefs about sin and about salvation. What does it mean to be a woman, and as a woman to name myself as made in the image of God? What might a feminist pastoral theology contribute to the question of the connections between gender and sexuality and God?

The third principle is that *the aim of feminist pastoral theology is to renew and to transform belief and practice.* Chapter 6, while still focused on the 'image of God', concentrates on the issue of women and the church. Despite the pain and hurt so often caused (which necessarily forms part of our discussion) the church remains a central locus of women's caring and being cared for, and indeed of feminist pastoral and theological reflection. Chronicling women's writing on pastoral theology, care and counselling in the past three decades Greider, Johnson and Leslie justify their 'primary contribution of a focus on *ekklesia* and its ministry' by pointing out that 'it reminds us that, for better as well as for worse, the identifying community and context for Christians is the church' (1999: 28). *Ekklesia* indicates those communities where 'unoppressive and caring ministries' are found, communities neither coextensive with 'the church' nor independent of it. Vision and hope for such communities transform and renew our practices of caring and our vision of God.

Finally Chapter 7 addresses women as carers and women as cared for. There are issues here about appropriate mutuality in care, about women's ability (or lack of ability) to tell their stories, about power and about the nature of love and emotional labour. What practices encourage flourishing and life, for those caring and for those cared for?

I have found the dialogue between feminism and pastoral theology to be rich and creative. Some of the readers of this book will be joining that dialogue for the first time. Others I hope will be stimulated to take new paths in the conversation (in agreement or in disagreement) and to set off on new and exciting tracks. The journey starts with the concrete situations of women's lives and their struggles to articulate these within both the practical and the academic locations of pastoral theology—'from academy, kitchen or sanctuary' (Graham: 1998). We move on to engage these realities and these struggles painfully and problematically in dialogue with Christian theology and traditions, reaching through to transformed and transforming practices, beliefs and hopes. The end of this particular journey is in our hopes for the transformation and the flourishing of our communities and of our caring. Such hopes, however fragile, are not necessarily 'vain hopes', or mere idealism. They are explored here as part of an active journeying to wholeness, of an encouragement to commitment and to the fragile but tenacious embodying of hope and of love.

Chapter One

Pastoral Theology:
Who Needs a Feminist Perspective?

For a start, women do. Then so do men and children. And, to be honest, so does the whole created order. One might even be so bold as to suggest that God does.

In her collection of textual resources for feminist theology (Ruether 1985a: 72) Rosemary Radford Ruether includes a piece written by Judith Plaskow in 1972, 'A Jewish Feminist Midrash on Lilith and Eve'. Plaskow delightfully tells the story of Lilith, banished from the garden for considering herself more than Adam's servant, of Eve finding her true self in sisterhood, at first nervously and then boldly, of Adam confused but willing to rethink, and finally of the God who 'must become what I will become'. Christian theology and practice have so often failed women, and in so doing have failed absolutely. Still so much theological talk, so much church talk, goes on as if the issues raised by women, with ever-increasing urgency in the last few decades, had never been raised. So many conferences, so many bibliographies, so much Christian teaching simply bypasses the cries and the silences, the experiences and the exclusions, the revelations and the confused questionings of the women who make up the major part of most Christian communities. The Christian churches, and Christian beliefs about God, go on as if these revelations and questions did not exist. This book is a testimony against such dishonesty and such blindness.

Before setting about the substantial task with an analysis of the violence which pervades and undergirds the patriarchal order in which human beings live, and to which we subjugate both the non-human creation and also 'God', I shall indicate the need and the scope of a feminist perspective on pastoral theology. Within the context of an overall need for theological reorientation, I shall address the specific area of *pastoral* theology. This, as I have outlined in the Introduction, involves particularly the areas of *love* and *care*, and of the *practices* of the Christian community, specifically as these are considered 'in terms of [or in relation to] God'. I shall do this by attending to three themes in this chapter: *the recent history of the feminist contribution to pastoral theology, the methodology of feminist pastoral theology, and an examination of the concepts and practices termed 'feminist'*.

By telling the history of women's contribution to pastoral theology, and more specifically of feminist analysis within pastoral theology, I hope to show that this perspective is a matter of great importance, which has until recently been neglected. It is of importance certainly to women and by extension to us all—pastoral caregivers, academics, ordained and lay persons, all members of the Christian community and beyond. By opening the methodological question I propose to show that we are not just talking about the content and the topics of what passes for pastoral theology, but about methods of action and reflection, about epistemology, about the nature of theology. It is not just a matter of what we know, but of *how* we know it; it is not just a matter of what we do, but of how we do it. Finally, by examining the concepts and practices termed 'feminist',[1] I will indicate that there is no monolithic 'feminist pastoral theology' but that feminism itself is an ever-moving concept with ever-moving practices, as indeed is pastoral theology itself. When the two are put together the result is something exceedingly mobile, hence very exciting. To wrestle with feminism and pastoral theology is to engage in a live and exhilarating debate. Feminist pastoral theology has a contribution to make to theological understanding, to feminist theory and to the practices of Christian communities.

The Feminist Contribution to Pastoral Theology

In May 1994 I attended one of the first Church of England services in which women were ordained to the priesthood. It was in Ely Cathedral. Several woman whom I knew closely were to be ordained, some after many years of faithful service and much bruising struggle, first as Deaconesses then as ordained Deacons. These women had been my friends; they had given me pastoral care, and I had given them pastoral care—in some cases as their college tutor.

> A priest is called by God...as servant and shepherd among the people to whom [s]he is sent... [S]he must set the Good Shepherd always before [her]...the treasure now to be entrusted to you is Christ's own flock... (*Alternative Service Book* of the Church of England 1980: 356).

1.   Some readers may prefer to look at this section of the chapter first, as it contains a definition of 'feminist'. This begins on page 28.

I didn't fancy myself much as a sheep. I felt insulted, and as if my pastoral care-giving of the past was not valued. Was I, by some operation of the Bishop's hands (or of the Holy Spirit) demoted to being a sheep? This incident raised for me sharply the issue that I later encountered in feminist and other critiques (Graham 1996: 49; Campbell 1981: 23) of a traditionally dominant image in pastoral theology, that of the shepherd and the sheep (Hiltner 1958; Tidball 1986). While there is much of value in this biblical image, it has been and is still used to foster paternalistic and dependent attitudes. What new paradigms of pastoral theology, what new images of ministry and of pastoral care has a feminist perspective to offer us?

This is not to say that all that we have inherited is useless from a feminist perspective. Jesus speaks of 'the householder who brings out of [her] treasure what is new and what is old' (Mt. 13.52). When I left my last job, as a tutor in an Anglican theological college (a teacher and a lay person training ordinands) it was this verse which my colleague read out when she presided at my final Eucharist. To me it was an empowering image of my ministry. More generally it offers a model for the project of this book—not only to find new treasures but also to renew the old. Rosemary Radford Ruether writes of searching for the 'shiny bits' of past tradition as part of our search for justice and healing (1995: 53). Just so may feminist pastoral theology search for new and old treasure.

Pastoral theology is a latecomer to the feminist theological scene. Only in the 1990s has a feminist perspective on pastoral theology received significant and sustained attention in publications in the field. This compares with some 40 years of contributions in biblical and other fields. Two important contributors to feminist pastoral theology have recently offered tentative suggestions as to why this might be so.

Elaine Graham refers to 'the twin syndromes of "sexism" and "clericalism"', pointing out that '[w]ithin a discipline dominated by an androcentric (male-dominated) clerical paradigm, women were offered little opportunity as non-male, non-ordained persons to be recognised as agents or clients of pastoral ministry' (1999a: 185 n. 3). Bonnie Miller-McLemore identifies 'proximity to the more conserving structures of congregations', the 'precariousness of the field itself and the potentially increased liabilities of adding feminism and womanism', and the similarity of some of the methodology of a feminist perspective to methods already espoused in pastoral theology, for example personal experience as a source of theological reflection (1999: 87). Miller-McLemore's suggestion that practical fields may attract conservative people and foster conservative practices, encouraged in the case of pastoral theology by the inherent conservatism of traditional congregational structures and ethos, is at first surprising.

Practitioners may be more inclined to action than to theory, and the interesting point here is that 'practice' (and by association 'action') not 'theory' is seen as inherently conservative. This is in contrast to the normal tendency in theology to associate 'theorizers' with the academic ivory tower and 'practitioners' with more radical engagement with experience and action.[2]

Recent Key Literature

At this point I have a suggestion for the reader. What follows in this chapter is a survey and a map of the current state of feminist pastoral theology. This contains important information and guidance to anyone studying feminist pastoral theology. However, those who are interested in the topic in a more informal way, or indeed those who are testing out whether they think the topic is of importance at all, may find it more helpful to turn at this point to Chapter 2 which gets straight to the heart of the issues, perhaps returning to Chapter 1 at a later stage.

As might be expected, the contributions from a feminist perspective to the literature of pastoral theology, care and counselling in this recent period have been more extensive in North America than in Britain. The important volume *Feminist and Womanist Pastoral Theology* (Miller-McLemore and Gill-Austern 1999), gives an assessment of the recent feminist contribution to pastoral theology. It contains both a comprehensive account of feminist and womanist contributions to the discipline and also creative engagement with ongoing debates within pastoral theology. The opening chapter by Kathleen J. Greider, Gloria A. Johnson and Kristen J. Leslie, 'Three Decades of Women Writing for our Lives', charts the growth and development of women's contributions to the field and highlights helpfully significant areas for consideration in feminist pastoral theology. These include 'a "communal contextual paradigm" of pastoral care' (p. 22, quoting Patton 1993) and 'seven foci in women's publications', namely *ekklesia* and its ministry, marginalized people and taboo topics, female experience, theological education, soulfulness, violence and systems of care.

It is significant that the words 'feminist' and 'womanist' are used as partners throughout this collection. Such collaboration in diversity is a methodological characteristic of feminist pastoral theology. In ch. 2 of *Feminist and Womanist Pastoral Theology*, 'A Womanist Search for Sources', Carroll Watkins Ali lays out well the 'womanist school of thought that had begun to develop in the scholarship of African American Women' (1999: 52) as this connects with

---

2.   A practitioner is not the same thing as an activist; the latter term normally implies a commitment to political and social change.

pastoral theology. Womanist theology is particularly associated with African American women, but 'womanist' is also a term appropriated by Black women more widely.[3]

The significance of this and other such collections is at least threefold. First, women's actual lives and even bodily experiences are recognized as worthy of serious consideration in pastoral care. Second, there is a question of view and method. These works do not treat women's experiences as a topic to be viewed from outside, but the viewpoint is the viewpoint of women, often writing about their own experiences. Finally, there is a serious attempt to engage the theological dimension from the perspective of women's experiences.[4]

Much more work, however, needs to be done in the area of theological reflection, and I intend that the present book will be a contribution to this project. I concur with the judgment of Elaine Graham concerning the recent 'trajectory of feminist critique and reconstruction' that:

> the actual processes of retrieval, reconstruction and renewal imply complex epistemological and hermeneutical considerations: attention to priorities concerning the sources and norms of authentic theological discourse which are not given sufficiently detailed attention (Graham 1999a: 199).

Graham's own work, as a British pastoral theologian, includes coeditorship of *Life Cycles: Women and Pastoral Care* (Graham and Halsey 1993), a work written by women reflecting on their life experiences, of singleness and of motherhood, of liturgy and of ministerial training, of caring and of social work, and a contribution to *Liberating Faith Practices: Feminist Practical Theologies in Context* (Ackermann and Bons-Storm 1998). Recently published by an international group of scholars in pastoral/practical theology, this book serves as 'a significant opportunity for the international theological community to assess…[W]hat, if anything, distinguishes practical theological scholarship from a feminist perspective' (Graham 1999a: 185). The work demonstrates an ongoing commitment to, and wrestling with, the three areas of significance I

---

3.   See Dixon (2000) for a British perspective.

4.   For example, Maxine Glaz and Jeanne Stevenson Moessner's edited volume *Women in Travail and Transition: A New Pastoral Care* (1991) is an early contribution to the foregrounding of women's experience as a source of methodological and theological reflection on pastoral care, dealing with such issues as abuse, depression and women's work. In 1996 Stevenson Moessner edited a further volume *Through the Eyes of Women: Insights for Pastoral Care* which extends the discussion to include, among other topics, anger, sexual identity and eating disorders. The recent work of Nancy Gorsuch *Introducing Feminist Pastoral Care and Counseling* (2001), was unfortunately not available to me at the time of completing this book.

have identified—women's actual experiences, questions of viewpoint and method, and the theological dimension.

It is Graham's particular contribution to feminist pastoral theology to wrestle systematically and in a determinedly sustained way with the *theological* question. In *Transforming Practice* (1996, see also 1999a: 208) she stakes out a claim for pastoral theology as critical attention to the 'purposeful practices of intentional communities', locating the theologically disclosive nature of practice in the value-laden practices of communities of faith. This is an attempt to engage the critique and the insights of a postmodern perspective, which takes seriously embodiment, performativity, provisionality, hermeneutical complexity and pluralism, in a theologically constructive proposal. It is a disturbing account to those whose faith perspectives require some kind of authenticated 'revealed' truth independent of practice. Such faith perspectives, however, cannot bypass the questions she raises if they are to offer convincing alternative accounts.

In a specifically feminist context her vision of practical wisdom goes beyond, without discarding, a liberationist account, and engages those aspects of feminism which might disturb such an account. For example, building on the work of the French feminist philosopher, Luce Irigaray, in which 'woman' and the divine are linked in an idea of the 'sensible transcendental', Graham opens up a notion of utopian sacred space (1999a: 203, 211) which encourages the imagination towards that which is different, divine, 'unfinished and unfixed'.[5] This brings discussion of what is meant by 'the divine' and how it is named into the heart of feminist pastoral theology. This theological question, and the underlying tension between a movement towards the themes of equality and a 'God beyond gender' on the one hand, and the exploration of the female/feminine and the 'divine feminine' on the other, will run like a thread through the subject matter of this book. Graham challenges us to think as rigorously about *theology* as about care and so offers an important contribution to contemporary pastoral theology. My intention is to work within this framework of priorities, bringing together *pastoral*, *feminist* and *theological* perspectives.

Critique and Reconstruction

Feminist theology as a whole, and feminist pastoral theology within it, has 'operated within a dynamic of *critique and reconstruction*' (Graham 1999a: 186). This process has embraced the practices and the theories of the academy, the

---

5.   This is reminiscent of, though also very different from, the 'Messianic endspace' found in the work of Ernst Bloch and taken up by Jürgen Moltmann.

caring professions and the church. A pattern which involves both critique and reconstruction (although not always found together in equal measure) can be traced in the work of feminist biblical scholars, systematic theologians, historians and practical/pastoral theologians. In the attempt to expose the ideological distortions of patriarchy and to build communities of flourishing for both women and men, attention has sometimes been paid to the ways in which women have been made *victims*, and at other times to the neglected *contributions* of women. Both perspectives are necessary. In particular it should be recognized that even where women have historically been creative agents, their marginalization from the history 'making' or writing has excluded and victimized them. That is why the discovering and writing of history is an essential part of the feminist project (Lerner 1986: 5). I shall deal with the area of women's writing and research in the section on methodology, after exploring three key areas of critique and reconstruction in pastoral theology: *topics and themes, subjectivity and agency, models and paradigms*. In fact the latter two themes are best treated together as issues interweave.

Topics and Themes

The emergence of feminist topics and themes once neglected in pastoral theology is clearly related to the presence of women's distinctive voices and perspectives in the academy and in pastoral practice, to the paradigm shifts in pastoral theology away from individualized and clericalized models, and to the progress of the feminist political and academic agenda in the secular world. Two fundamentally important themes which have emerged are the theme of violence and abuse, and the theme of the body or embodiment.

1. *Violence and abuse.* Religious communities have condoned and perpetrated violence by their teachings and by the actions of those in power within them. This makes the topic one of urgent importance for pastoral theology, and constitutes a strong reason for starting my own analysis with the topic in Chapter 2. Violence and abuse are not only evils which need to be combated externally by church and religious communities, but they must be named and combated *within* church and religious communities. It is only recently that such topics have come to public attention as a serious problem for society.

> The higher profile afforded to the issue of male violence against women in recent years is almost entirely due to the political practice of activists in the women's liberation movement and feminist research deriving from this. Until the early 1970s little was known or written about such violence, and scant attention was paid to it as a social problem (Maynard 1993: 100).

Greider, Johnson and Leslie (1999: 43) identify violence against women and children as the topic which has indisputably received the most attention from women publishing in pastoral theology, care and counselling between 1983 and mid-1998, beginning with Marie Marshall Fortune's *Sexual Violence: The Unmentionable Sin* (1983). Response to these issues takes a practical as well as a research and a reflective form, as demonstrated in the centre Fortune herself founded in 1977—the 'Center for the Prevention of Sexual and Domestic Violence'—and in the pioneering work of Lesley Orr MacDonald, 'Out of the Shadows: Christianity and Violence against Women in Scotland'—a project under the auspices of the Centre for Theology and Public Issues in Edinburgh.

Violence and abuse against women is a global phenomenon. The contributors to *Women Resisting Violence*, published in 1996 as the result of an international dialogue instigated by the Women's Commission of the Ecumenical Association of Third World Theologians, name the following interconnected forms of violence against women: cultural, ecological, domestic, physical, economic and military violence (Mananzan *et al.* 1996). It is an important task of feminist pastoral theology to unearth, analyse, denounce and work against such violence. In this task pastoral theologians will need to examine in a self-critical way their own theologies and their own church communities, because violence is not just a problem 'out there'.[6]

2. *Embodiment*. The theme of 'embodiment' has clear links to the topic of violence. It has become a central theme across a variety of philosophical and theological discussions, especially those rooted in a postmodern perspective. In the context of pastoral theology it serves to focus attention on a wide range of topics, for example, motherhood, lesbianism, eating disorders, fashion, ecology, representation of women in art, menstruation, rape. The 'body' and 'body theology' are rooted in some of the key doctrines and practices of the Christian faith—for example incarnation and Eucharist—as an earlier volume in this series points out (Isherwood and Stuart 1998: 16). Embodiment furthermore points not only to the incarnational but also the performative nature of theology and to the need for interpretive awareness of social construction and attendant issues of ideology—'our experience of ourselves as "body-selves" is

---

6.   As a follow up to the Decade of Churches in Solidarity with Women, the World Council of Churches has launched a 'Decade to Overcome Violence 2001–2010'; those interested in associating themselves with a theological network to resource this work are asked to contact Lesley Orr MacDonald and Helen Hood, DOV, Room 5, Annie Small House, 18 Inverleith Terrace, Edinburgh EH3 5NS, Scotland, UK; tel. +44 131 332 0881; fax +44 131 332 0804; e-mail: wcc.dov-women@ecosse.net

never innocent of social construction or unmarked by the constraints of power and difference' (Graham 1999c: 79).

To pay attention to ourselves as embodied selves expands the range of pastoral theological interest. It also provides a methodological tool to critique the inadequate views of personhood and bodiliness with which much Christian theology operates. Attention to our bodies furthermore invites an exploration of the basis of epistemology. 'Knowing' happens through our bodies as well as our minds.[7]

Violence and embodiment point to fundamental structures of historical human existence, and particularly historical female existence. They are therefore important themes for feminist pastoral theology. Such themes affect reflection and practice within the traditional areas of pastoral care (such as illness or family breakdown) and also on a wider front, including, for example, liturgy (Procter-Smith 1995a) and the theological virtue of love (Bennett Moore 1998a; Gill-Austern 1996). Writing in the field of feminist pastoral theology reaches into ever-increasing spheres of ever more diverse women's experience. As Bonnie Miller-McLemore writes, 'feminist pastoral theology involves extensive engagement with particular thematic practices or topics, placing them within a broader panorama of psychological, cultural, and theological critique and reformulation' (1999: 89). This topical reconstruction, within a wide interdisciplinary horizon, is a key contribution of feminist pastoral theology.

Subjectivity and Agency; Models and Paradigms
1. *Pastoral persons.* I mentioned earlier my problem with sheep and shepherds, a problem which highlights both the question of agency and the question of models. A feminist perspective rejects models that are individualist, elitist and authoritarian, and seeks to expand subjectivity and agency within a communal paradigm of shared power. The most serious critique of the 'shepherd' image is therefore not that it is outmoded and irrelevant to much modern life, but that it has been associated with, and may tend to perpetuate, an inappropriate model of pastoral care. Such a model sees the individual carer, a professional and possibly an ordained person, as the protector, guide, decision-maker and authoritative expert within a pastoral situation. The fact that such individuals have in history normally been (and often still are) men, exacerbates the problem for women. Women wish to be acknowledged and taken seriously both as recipients and as agents of pastoral care. This acknowledgment needs to go

---

7.   Melanie May's *A Body Knows* is a particularly striking example of such an exploration of bodily knowing (May 1995).

beyond the stereotyping of women as needy, weak and neurotic recipients of pastoral care on the one hand, or women as by nature loving and caring on the other. A model of pastoral theology as reflection on the intentional practices of the whole Christian (or other religious) community is much more helpful, taking into account as it does the activities and values of the whole community and seeking out pastoral agency in a wide variety of practices and across a wide spectrum of both individuals and groups (Graham 1996: 204; 1999b: 452).

A similar feminist critique has been made of the clerical paradigm in pastoral theology. This critique is helpful in so far as it reinforces the importance of community, of mutuality and of the need to move away from inappropriately hierarchical models. We must, however, be careful not to lose the best import of the clerical and indeed the shepherd models in one crucial respect—the focus on the care and love of God mediated through human beings to the human community. Miller-McLemore rightly criticises the jettisoning of the clerical paradigm when this brings a move away from care and towards the academy, away from 'the messiness of human suffering, the ambiguities and subjectivity of faith claims and spiritual experiences, and the complications of ministerial practices of transformation' (1999: 93). We must acknowledge the real sense in which members of the community exercise a ministry of particular love and care, and of leadership in love and care, for which shepherding is not yet a dead metaphor within the Christian tradition.

2. *Pastoral action.* The influential definition of pastoral care as 'healing, sustaining, guiding and reconciling' (Clebsch and Jaekle 1975) identifies core elements which make good sense within a 'shepherding' model. While not rejecting these elements, feminist pastoral theologians seek to expand the range of core pastoral practices as seen within a 'communal contextual paradigm'. 'Resisting, empowering, nurturing and liberating' are suggested by Miller-McLemore[8] (1999: 80).

Resisting points to the work of exposing and standing up against patriarchy and all its works. The precise form this takes is culturally determined, but resistance to violence and sexual abuse in all its forms is central. Resisting is painful and much feminist pastoral theology is created from a place of pain and resistance; for an excellent example see Heather Walton's article 'Passion and Pain: Conceiving Theology out of Infertility' (Walton 1998).

Empowering points to the need for an analysis of power relationships that unmasks the hidden ways in which women and other 'submerged groups' are disempowered in social and pastoral relationships. The advent of a more

---

8.   She builds here on the work of Carroll Watkins Ali.

sophisticated deconstruction of the operations of power, which no longer relies on a straightforward oppressor/ oppressed model, should not blind us to the need to understand the various ways in which groups and individuals are indeed disempowered. A particular form that the empowerment of women has often taken in pastoral care and theology is simply listening—listening to women's stories and 'listening into speech' those who cannot even tell their stories.

Nurturing is a dangerous word, filled with possibilities of valuing and struggling for that which makes for human flourishing, but fraught with dangers from the biological essentialism and the ideological constructions which confine women to the private world, to the less prestigious caring roles, to 'women's work'.

Liberating indicates a commitment that binds feminist pastoral theology to other theologies of liberation, rooted in real life, in justice issues, in a concern for the structural as well as the individual, in the prophetic role of the church (Lartey 1997: 37). The concerns of feminist pastoral theology with the well-being of women cannot be divorced from the concerns of all who fight against discrimination whether on grounds of ethnicity, sexual orientation, disability or class. Nor is the flourishing of the non-human creation to be ignored, as the serious contribution of a number of ecofeminist theologians indicates (Ruether in Mananzan *et al.* 1996).

3. *Pastoral context*. Anton Boisen's expression 'the living human document' as a description of the 'text' or subject matter of pastoral theology has been immensely influential and creative.[9] To call a person and their situation a 'document' is to draw attention to the need for interpretation and understanding. Although this image has been recently taken up 'as standing for the pastoral encounter or event in its widest context' (Graham 1999b: 453), some feminist pastoral theologians prefer to use the image of a web to draw attention to that wider context in which all living humans are enmeshed. Bonnie Miller-McLemore suggests the metaphor 'living human web' as indicative of a shift 'to a focus on care understood as part of a wide cultural, social, and religious context' (Miller-McLemore 1996: 14). Such a shift in focus not only points towards the ways in which individuals cannot be seen independently of their social context, it also highlights the necessity for pastoral theology to be part of a web of scholarship and analysis involving a wide range of disciplines—the social sciences, fine arts, literature. It is important for the future of pastoral theology, including feminist pastoral theology, that as it moves from a 'professional cap-

---

9. For a discussion of this metaphor and sources see Miller-McLemore 1996: 16.

tivity' within a predominantly therapeutic model (Campbell 1985: 40), it does not succumb instead to a captivity to the social sciences. Liturgy, creative writing, art and music are forms for the forging and the expression of pastoral theology—forms whose creative and symbolic power should not be lost in an enthusiasm for the language of the social sciences or the information gathered through empirical research.

If the metaphor of the web conjures up the importance and diversity of context and methods in pastoral theology, it also points to a way of knowing and understanding. Webs are connected with spiders. The spider image is a good one for expressing a certain way of learning. Martha Nussbaum, in *The Fragility of Goodness*, refers to:

> [A] spider sitting in the middle of its web, able to feel and respond to any tug in any part of the complicated structure… The image of learning expressed in this style…stresses responsiveness and and attention to complexity; it discourages the search for the simple and, above all, for the reductive (1986: 69).

Nussbaum is writing of the making of moral choices in the face of the complexities of living. The pastoral agent is such a learner and is faced with such choices. This is a picture of 'a watcher, a burrower, a spider in a web feeling the tug, an agent embedded in circumstances in which attention and responsiveness…are key values' (Bennett Moore 1997–98: 39).

This image of a web is an appropriate way to draw to a close the consideration of models and agency in feminist pastoral theology. It highlights well the sense in which the feminist contribution is not only about deconstruction of models and practices but about creative reconstruction. This is an appropriate point to move to the next phase in the consideration of feminist perspectives on pastoral theology, that is to consider questions of methodology.

The Methodology of Feminist Pastoral Theology

Methodology in feminist pastoral theology, as has already been indicated, shares features with other kinds of pastoral theology. Clearly the key distinguishing feature is its commitment to a feminist perspective in the sense of foregrounding the experiences and needs, stories and voices of women, in the context of an analysis of the patriarchal nature of society. More, however, may be said by way of delineating the common or usual features of feminist pastoral theological methods. The following features should be seen as significant. Feminist pastoral theology starts with practice, not with theory; is mutual, not paternalistic or clerical; is gender sensitive and eschews sexism; is political and structural, not individualistic; is pluralist and dialogical, not authoritarian. Feminist pastoral theology is an advocacy theology, but also values critical reflection; the tension set up by these two commitments will be explored.

The question of epistemology is also central. The methodology of feminist pastoral theology is about practical commitments; it is also about truth and how we come to know it. So, before briefly introducing the features just mentioned, I want to take a look at the character of feminist research and writing in pastoral theology.

Feminist Research and Writing
A distinctive feature of feminist pastoral theology is the form its research and writing takes. Perhaps this would be best described as a set of distinctive features, features held in common with much other feminist research and writing. It would be wrong to suggest that no other work in pastoral theology shares these characteristics, but taken together they are distinctive of a feminist perspective and commitment.

Collaboration. The most immediately striking characteristic of much feminist work is its collaborative nature. A high proportion of recently published work in the field comprises edited collections.[10] These are normally quite deliberately composed in a collaborative manner, in order to highlight certain values and in assurance of the worthwhile gains of such a project. Miller-McLemore speaks of a *web* of women's writing:

> Our united effort defies mathematical and empirical logic that contends that '1+1=2'. One plus one becomes something entirely new, different, and more than the mere summation of its parts. Our shared meals, correspondence, phone calls, and late-night hotel room conversations affirm a religious truth that 'where two or three are gathered in my name, I am there among them' (Mt. 18.20) (1996: 23).

Moessner writes in the Introduction to that same collection, 'This cooperative effort challenges by example the academic guild's tendency to be as monolithic as the culture it critiques' (1996: 3). This type of collaboration takes seriously not only diversity of viewpoint but also of social location, as exemplified by the volume *Feminist and Womanist Pastoral Theology* where students and faculty members and African American and European American women research and write chapters cooperatively (Miller-McLemore 1999: 15).

---

10. See Ackermann and Bons-Storm 1998; Glaz and Moessner 1991; Graham and Halsey 1993; Miller-McLemore and Gill-Austern 1999; Moessner 1996.

Personal Commitment. Feminist pastoral theology is further characterized by its commitment to 'that which promotes the full humanity of women' (Ruether 1983: 18). This commitment defines both content and method. It is both a theoretical ethical position and an intention towards action. In this commitment to change on behalf of those who are oppressed or undervalued feminist pastoral theology shares a position common to various liberation theologies, and to versions of the 'pastoral cycle' of reflection and action which support them (Ballard and Pritchard 1996).

Closely allied to commitment is the personal involvement which characterizes feminist pastoral theology. This is not just a question of familiarity with the subject matter, or of personal experience of pastoral care which issues in reflection. It is a question about epistemology—about understanding and the ability to voice that understanding. Liz Stanley and Sue Wise (1993) put provocatively on the agenda of feminist social research that research must be intimately connected with a person's own experience:

> We believe that a feminist social science should begin with the recognition that 'the personal', direct experience, underlies all behaviours and actions. We need to find out what it is that we know and what it is that we experience. We need to reclaim, name and rename our experiences and our knowledge of the social world we live in and daily construct (1993: 164).

Stanley and Wise's contention forces us to consider both the way in which things might be truly known, and also the ethical question concerning who has the right to speak or claim knowledge on behalf of anyone but themselves, and what way such claims and such speaking might be responsible. It is also important to consider how our own 'knowing' is conditioned and partial. As Lorraine Code says, 'knowing well is a matter of considerable moral significance' (1987: 3). Feminist research in pastoral theology will take seriously the 'situatedness' of the knower, including her personal commitments.

Women's Experience. All that has been said thus far presupposes what has traditionally been seen as the prime characteristic of feminist theology, including feminist pastoral theology, which is its commitment to the primacy of women's experience as a starting point for reflection and as a criterion for evaluation. This practice, and the theoretical and practical problems which it raises, will form a central strand of the explorations in this book. I therefore do no more than note the point here.

Ambiguous Location in the Academy. Research and writing in feminist pastoral theology is often characterized by its ambiguous relationship to the academy and the 'scholarly guilds'. Mary Grey has spoken of feminist theology as the 'changeling in the academy' (1993). While some feminist pastoral theologians hold senior positions in universities and in seminaries, the ambiguity demonstrated in Moessner's words about challenging the academic guild is mirrored in research and working practices. Collaborative working practices and publication, commitment to creative discussion and to teaching in the face of the pressure to 'publish or perish', the value accorded to story, to art and to other modes of self expression not traditional in the academy, the pressures of pastoral care itself, including the disproportionate burden of pedagogical pastoral care exercised by women, all bring feminist pastoral theologians into that same ambiguous relationship to the academy felt by feminist academics in all disciplines. In the case of pastoral theology the continually contested status and identity of pastoral theology itself exacerbate the ambiguity and liminality of this position:

> why would one choose further marginalisation in a field that already suffers that plight? Adding feminist theory to pastoral theology renders its position even more precarious as a discipline poised between practice, person, confessional religious congregations, and the academy (Miller-McLemore 1999: 87).

Suspicion and Silence. While ambiguity characterizes the position of many feminist pastoral theologians, suspicion must characterize all feminist pastoral theology. Suspicion of the dominant sociocultural, psychological, philosophical and theological narratives should inform all feminist pastoral care and theological reflection, including research and writing.[11] This position is familiar to us both from the great Enlightenment 'masters of suspicion'—Freud, Marx, Nietzsche—and from the postmodern suspicion of any 'grand narrative'. The particular contours this suspicion takes in feminist pastoral theology are given their form by a social analysis which sees an understanding of the pervasive presence of patriarchy as foundational, and by a realization of the near impossibility of women being able to articulate their experience and story given the dominant forms of narrative available. The depth of this problem is clearly demonstrated in Bons-Storm's case studies of women's inability to tell their 'truth' in the pastoral encounter, dogged as they are by silence, by 'unstory' (apparent falsehood which is indicative of a truth for which there are no words or concepts), by the 'rhetoric of uncertainty', and by dominant social narratives which constrain and damage. Luce Irigaray, building on the work of psychoanalyst Jacques Lacan, explores the depth dimensions of this silence, this inability of women to find language, in terms of a more pervasive 'lack' associated

---

11. For a trenchant and lively presentation of this case see Riet Bons-Storm, *The Incredible Woman* (1996).

with women.[12] Mary Daly's idiosyncratic use of language[13] is a further and quite different response to the same underlying issue: 'I just could not find all the Words I needed in the standard old toms' tomes' (Daly 1993: 292).

Bons-Storm's pastoral theology, Irigaray's philosophy and Mary Daly's theology all challenge us to see that any significant progress towards women's being able to 'speak' their truth will require a reassessment of how we conceive and speak of the 'divine'. This conviction underlies the attention in Chapters 4 to 6 of this book to the question of the 'image of God'. The questions feminist theology asks about women are also questions about God. As in Plaskow's midrash God 'must become who I will become'.

In relation to research and writing in feminist pastoral theology this question mark over the possibility of women's being able to 'speak their truth' must be taken with the utmost seriousness. Stanley and Wise's caution that we may not presume to speak for others must be taken further; in what sense can we even speak for ourselves? The feminist pastoral theologian does not escape the bind in which all women are caught.

Features of Feminist Pastoral Theological Method

Practice. There are, roughly speaking, three possible models of doing pastoral theology. The first is to start from the 'authorized' tradition, whether represented by church tradition or by the Bible, and from this make deductions about appropriate practice. This is essentially an 'applied theology' model. The second is to engage the theological tradition on the one hand, and current practice and experience on the other, in a dialogue in which both theology and practice are potentially open to mutual transformation as a result. This method is variously referred to, depending on the exact form it takes and on its starting point, as 'critical correlation', or 'the pastoral cycle', or a 'praxis' method of doing theology (Ballard and Pritchard 1996: 58-68). The third model focuses on practice itself, which is seen as the primary or indeed the sole means of access to truth. So pastoral theology becomes the interrogation of the intentional practices of Christian communities to unearth core values and beliefs and to bring these into dialogue with the core values and beliefs of other people and other groups (Graham 1996). There is what may be called a 'hard' and a 'soft' version of this model. The 'hard' version says there is no 'transcendent' or 'authorized' truth, only the values we construct. The 'soft' version says that human beings can only gain access to transcendent truth via the practices of

---

12. For a clear presentation of Irigaray's work in the context of pastoral theology see Graham 1999a: 201-204.

13. See especially *Webster's First New Intergalactic Wickdary of the English Language* 1988.

communities. Graham's insistence that pastoral theology, as the interrogation of the value-laden intentional practices of the Christian community, is 'theologically disclosive' (1996: 10) suggests to me the 'soft' version. Her view of pastoral theology is 'not a surrender to nihilism, but a recognition that "truth" is incarnated in the performative, embodied practices of intentional communities' (Graham 1999a: 208).

Of these three models feminist pastoral theologians tend to prefer the second and third, although there are feminist theologians, such as Elaine Storkey (Storkey 2000) who take seriously feminist questions in the context of a primary commitment to the first model. The radical nature of the questions and the ideological critique directed to the Christian tradition, including the Bible, together with a strong emphasis on women's experience, mean that the very notion of the 'authorized' is itself made problematic in a feminist perspective.

The starting point in practice, and in particular those practices engaged in and experienced by women, gives feminist pastoral theology certain contours. 'Practice' is a complex idea, as can be illustrated by thinking through how we understand practice in the context of the well-known phenomenon 'piano practice'. Practice can immediately be seen as something involving repetition, learning and performance, a complex interaction of interpretation of a tradition of practices, tension between faithfulness and innovation, involving a definition of 'perfection' which is constructed but flexible and even, arguably, 'given'. Piano playing is most certainly embodied understanding.

Likewise within a feminist understanding of pastoral practice the importance of cultural context and shaping and of the history of practices is acknowledged; women's practices vary widely. Subjectivity is valued as well as objectivity; indeed the sharp division between them is blurred. Values and truths are seen as interim and self-reflexive. Knowledge is understood as 'situated' (Code 1991; Haraway 1991) and embodied.

Piano playing also involves performance. The traditional duo of biological essentialism and social constructionism beloved of feminists in their analysis of women's experience should be supplemented by the notion of gender as *performed* (Butler 1990: 139). This expresses a crucial understanding. That which we do is not just an expression of how we are constituted biologically, or of how we have been constructed socially; it is also purposive and creative. We take an active part in practices: 'bodies are creative agents as well as socially constructed objects' (Graham 1999c: 83). This may be in a transgressive way, for example, in drag gender is deliberately 'performed' and performed transgressively; or it may be in a conformist way, as in the ways my mother's generation performed the roles of 'good wife and mother' in conformity to social expectations. But they did 'perform', and often interestingly and creatively; they were not *mere* slaves of their bodily 'nature' or the way society constructed their role. This emphasis on agency is important for a pastoral theology that seeks to maximize women's understanding of their own subjectivity and actions.

While the importance of practice as a starting point must not be overlooked it is crucial to bear in mind the already mentioned inherent potential conservatism of practice and practitioners. Theory is not only the place of 'authoritative' instruction 'from above'; it can also be the place of questioning, of the subversion of the 'common sense', the place where we can say ' but it doesn't have to be like this, let's try another way of thinking about it'. This is the place of theory in the 'left-wing' disciplines. It is most important to bear this in mind in pastoral theological education. While new theory arises from experience, particularly experience of dissonance or suffering, an overconcentration on the 'reflective practitioner' aspect of pastoral theology can easily topple into a 'how can we do this better' mentality, which does not see the more radical questions.

Such theorizing may take place in a classroom context. Theological education is as important a facet of pastoral theology as congregational care.[14] Feminist pedagogy is an integral part of feminist pastoral theology. *How* we teach and learn, how staff–student relationships are worked out, how assessment takes place, are as important in feminist education as the *content* of what is learned and taught.[15] But theorizing doesn't only happen in the classroom. I am fascinated by bell hooks's account of theorizing when as a child she managed to escape her father's violence and her mother's acceptance of it into 'a place of sanctuary in "theorising", in making sense out of what was happening. I found a place where I could imagine possible futures, a place where life could be lived differently' (hooks 1994: 61). To understand the connections between theory and fantasy is to see the imaginative and the radical dimensions of theory, and to give it its rightful place with practice and experience— not as the starting point but as the means beyond the inadequacies, and worse, of current practice and experience. It is also to see clearly how theory is not an end in itself but a spur to bring about change. Such an understanding shows also the place of storytelling in feminist theological method, both as a means of describing reality and as a way of spinning 'fantasy' or 'theory' in order to open up new possibilities.

14. See Miller-McLemore and Gill-Austern (1999: 14), Greider, Johnson and Leslie (1999: 36).

15. For more detailed discussion of feminist pedagogy see Bennett Moore (1997–98; 1998b; 2002a).

Mutuality. Feminist pastoral theology prizes mutuality, empowerment and the supported holding of responsibility, and is suspicious of overemphasis on clerical or individualistic therapeutic paradigms. The 'whole systems' elements in pastoral situations are emphasized, whether these be families, social structures, underlying cultural assumptions or economic conditions. Healing is seen not as something brought to the needy individual by the pastoral expert, but as happening within a context and with strong elements of mutuality. The language of healing must not lead to an individualistic view in which the sufferer is enabled to adjust to reality at the expense of the questioning of the conditions and context that cause the suffering.

A feminist approach emphasizes the ways in which pastoral help may be received as well as given, and also will normally involve a wide network of giving and receiving across time and space. However, emphasis on the mutuality and contextual complexity of the pastoral encounter must not be at the expense of losing the sense in which all individual persons can at specific times be agents of care and of love in specific ways, which may at least *pro tempore* have a distinctly one-sided nature.

Asking the Gender Question. Sensitivity to the issue of gender is *prima facie* a characteristic of feminist pastoral theological method. Almost all areas of pastoral theology are illuminated by asking the question, 'How does a gender perspective affect this issue?' The first fundamental question concerns what subjects are considered proper to pastoral theology. The recent history of publications in feminist pastoral theology is in itself a testimony to the rich variety of subject matter to do with women's lives and women's bodies which has been put on the agenda by feminist pastoral theologians. But the gender question is more than a matter of *what* is looked at; it is a question of *how* those issues are looked at. The two most important factors are the illumination of that which is hidden through an analysis of the distortions of patriarchy (such as hidden power relations or suppressed perspectives and information) and the giving of a voice to women so that women's own concerns and perspectives can be heard.

Analysis of patriarchy in the context of feminist pastoral theology will illuminate not only those structures of society which it is the concern of feminism in general to expose, but particularly those patriarchal distortions that affect the believing community. This may take the form of the scrutiny of material and social relations between persons in a pastoral context to illuminate the dynamics of the power relationships. Such relationships may include elements of 'double identity' in which one and the same person may be powerful in some ways and weak in others (Billman 1996: 16). Specifically the question of sexuality, and of how the power that derives from the sexed and gendered nature of our relationships impinges on pastoral relationships, is of crucial importance (Rutter 1989). Individual relationships must always be analysed in the context of the wider social beliefs and practices in which they take place. Such analysis must also address the effect of doctrines and beliefs, of symbols and metaphors, as they are articulated onto the material practices of the church and the believing community. For example, what happens to the theological motif of 'self-sacrifice' when it is joined to the already existing patriarchal structures within families and churches and applied to women? (Bennett Moore 1998a) These concerns form much of the subject matter of this book, as the theoretical and methodological perspectives of this chapter are developed in relation to the realities of women's lives and of pastoral ministry.

Giving women a voice involves the creation of a safe context, the questioning of dominant sociocultural roles and other stereotypes (women as hysterical, needy, dependent) and helping women to find a language in which to tell their story. Bons-Storm's description of women's silence in pastoral counselling which I introduced earlier is corroborated in other work, for example the silence which Mary Belenky and her colleagues identify as characterizing some women's attempts to articulate what they know (Belenky *et al*. 1986). There are similar silences which Slee identifies in relation to women's attempts to describe their spirituality (Slee 2001) or Gilligan in relation to expressing their moral understanding (Gilligan 1993). The connections between silence and violence will be further explored in Chapter 2.

A gendered approach eschews an essentialist or universalist model of personhood, seeing groups and individuals in all their historical contingency, making connections and exposing differences, embracing plurality, multiplicity and complexity. While avoiding a simplistic division between women and men which would generate a further set of universals—'woman' and 'man'—a gendered approach in feminist pastoral theology has led in some circles to a concern for men's issues, in the realization that the issues raised for both sexes impinge directly and intimately on one another (Pryce 1996; Neuger and Poling 1997). Mark Pryce articulates the connections well:

> Men have lived for generations by the fictions which the women writers are re-writing. The new fictions are strange for men, they may even be painful. It is not easy for us to hear the voices of women, particularly if they articulate what challenges us. To listen to women is to risk change and even transformation (1996: 17).

The 'Different Voice': Justice, Diversity and Advocacy. Since feminist pastoral theologians seek to understand the experiences of women in their cultural and structural context, it follows that feminist pastoral theology is concerned to interpret and to act within the political and the structural perspective. In this its natural 'neighbours' in pastoral theology are the liberationist perspectives (Couture and Hunter 1995; Lartey 1997). The divide between the public and the private is broken down; 'the personal is political', whether this is seen primarily in relation to economics as in Marxist feminism, or primarily in relation to symbolism, language and sexuality, as in radical feminism.

Justice is therefore an important concept and value in feminist pastoral theology. Ethics based on justice may, however, tend towards a cold calculation of rights and wrongs, or may neglect complex factors of relationship and care. I vividly remember an ethics class in which the neat setting out by the tutor of lists of competing rights of mother and child in relation to abortion was totally subverted. A mature woman student, asked on what basis she had advised her pregnant daughter in this matter, said stumblingly and slowly, 'Well...in the end it came down to the kind of person she was'. While this 'different voice' gives important insight, a feminist approach will look also to wider structural and political issues. The emphasis on an ethic of care as a counterbalance to an ethic of justice in feminist theological ethics must not be transported into feminist pastoral theology in such a way as to lose the strong dimension of seeking justice (Gilligan 1993; Held 1995). For feminist pastoral theology justice and care are equally important.

Feminist pastoral theology is pluralist and dialogical in its approach to seeking truth, rather than reliant on monolithic authoritarian sources. Interdisciplinarity is characteristic of feminist pastoral theology, as it is of Women's Studies in general. Truth is seen as interim and reflexive, being found in the dialogue between different stories and different perspectives. This is not to fall into a valueless relativism. Rather it is to agree with Janet Martin Soskice that 'the truth looks different from here' (Soskice 1993) and to recognize 'otherness' of perspective as a means towards the truth and justice which we seek communally. In speaking of the 'other', pastoral theology at its best does not categorize, project onto and stereotype 'others' (in a diabolical reversal of the stereotyping which women refuse for themselves) but looks at and listens to the 'concrete other' (Benhabib 1992)—the other in all his or her particularity. Such a dialogue between different persons and groups opens the way to an understanding of truth and a way of doing justice which takes proper account of difference. Clearly this kind of dialogue presupposes that some kind of shared coherent meaning is possible and that it is meaningful to use the category 'human'. Neither of these assumptions are totally self-authenticating today (Mudge 1999), but they are normally made, and sometimes defended, implicitly or explicitly in feminist and other pastoral theology with reference to gender, cultural and other differences (Bons-Storm 1996; Lartey 1997). Chapter 5 will examine this issue further.

Some sort of self-reflexive hermeneutic of suspicion and criticism must be maintained in order to engage properly in a critical analysis. Many feminist pastoral theologians (who are often also pastoral practitioners) find that this sits in tension with the very nature of feminist theology, which, like all liberation theologies, is an advocacy theology. This is a dilemma in feminist epistemology and in feminist writing. In the rush of enthusiasm for the understanding which a critique of patriarchy brings to so much painful and hitherto unexplained experience, in the heady commitment to 'the promotion of the full humanity of women', it is easy to forget that there is also a critique of every kind of feminism to be made (West 1995). What is needed is a critical commitment, open-eyed and open-hearted. This recognition of the potential for diversity and critique within feminist pastoral theology leads naturally on to an examination of what is meant precisely by 'feminist' in this context.

An Examination of the Concepts and Practices Termed Feminist

What is Feminism?
bell hooks defines feminism as follows:

> Feminism is a struggle to end sexist oppression. Its aim is not to benefit solely any specific group of women, any particular race or class of women. It does not privilege women over men. It has the power to transform in a meaningful way all our lives (1984: 26).

As with Ruether's definition of feminist theology ('that which promotes the full humanity of women') it is not a question of privileging women over men, but of including women in the places where hitherto they have been excluded and transforming those places by their inclusion. Theological reflection on God and on humanity has for the most part in Christian history excluded the experiences and perspectives of women, and it is the business of feminist theology to put right this distortion in the interests of both women and men.

Put thus it is hard to see why any person of goodwill should not count themselves a feminist, unless they were to believe there is no such thing as sexist oppression or that women have not been excluded (in other words, that the analysis of society and church as patriarchal is inaccurate). The fact remains that in teaching feminist pastoral theology I find an enormous reluctance to embrace the word 'feminist' amongst colleagues and students. This is normally expressed as a reluctance to become a 'one-issue person' or to be woman-identified to the exclusion of men. This may indicate that the *practices* of feminists do not always fit neatly into the definitions above. There is, I believe, a further less frequently acknowledged factor, which is that once a feminist understanding has been embraced *nothing* remains sacred or untouched—no relationship, no belief about God, no text that we read, no everyday task. Our sexuality, our religion, our work, our thinking, all are touched. It is common for students (especially women) halfway through the 'Feminist Perspectives on Pastoral Theology' module to go through a period of confusion, even depression, and reorientation.

It is crucial to see that a 'feminist analysis' is not the same thing as 'women's experience'. A *feminist* analysis implies both the acceptance of the patriarchal nature of society and the commitment to change it. Women's experiences, and the narratives in which women tell these experiences and construct their identities (Chopp 1995; Bons-Storm 1996), are essential to a feminist analysis and to feminist pastoral theology. Three levels of working can be identified: the first is the level of experience, the description of what happens in experience and in practice; the second is the level of reflection on that experience and practice; the third is the level of reflection on methodology itself, and this is important in interdisciplinary studies such as pastoral theology and Women's Studies (Doehring 1999: 100; Hogan 1995).

The Problem of 'Women's Experience'
Furthermore, the category of 'women's experience' is in itself extremely problematic. As Elaine Graham says, '[w]omen's experience as a foundational category of feminism became deeply problematic in its tendency to become reified and universalised' (Graham 1996: 193). Over the last decade or so feminist theologians have moved to a much more sophisticated awareness of the diversity, the multiplicity and even the fragmentation of women's experiences. This is partly due to the multiplicity of voices which are now being heard, and in particular the challenge of Black 'womanist' theologians in North America and of Third World women theologians. It is also due to the theoretical perspectives of postmodernism and poststructuralist feminism.

The first volume of *Searching the Scriptures*, a major contribution to feminist biblical interpretation edited by Elisabeth Schüssler Fiorenza (1993b), refers to 'charting interpretation from different sociohistorical locations' and includes essays from womanist, *mujerista*, Asian and African scholars. Attention is paid in particular to the challenge from African American women, 'womanists' after the expression 'womanish' found in the works of Alice Walker, that white feminism has been historically tainted by racist attitudes, and by no means has represented the interests of Black American women. Not only have women's experiences differed, they have actually been fragmented and in conflict with one another. An example of this in a British context is Angela West's (1995) description of the breakdown of sisterhood among the Greenham Common peace women, partly over issues of race. The dominance of white Western, often middle-class, feminist theology is rightly challenged by a more global perspective which takes account of issues of race, poverty and cultural context and resists any attempt to universalize 'women's experience' from one socio-historical location. The recent publication of *Feminist and Womanist Pastoral Theology* (Miller-McLemore and Gill-Austern 1999) in America is a sign that at least in one context women pastoral theologians are able to work together from multiple perspectives; interestingly the editors identify the metaphors of 'bridge' and 'portage' as running throughout the book (p. 12). Less happy was the experience of the authors of *Liberating Faith Practices* (Ackermann and Bons-Storm 1998) who failed to engage a fully representative international community in their project, despite serious efforts to do so (p. 3).

Different Feminisms

It is now recognized that not only is there a multiplicity of voices which need to be heard and to engage one another, but that each group and indeed each individual has multiple identities in relation to issues of power and context. For example, womanist theologians have stressed the way in which Black women are doubly disempowered, both as women and as Black; white women, how-ever, are empowered as white and disempowered as female. Once factors of social status, economics, sexual orientation and so on are added in the picture becomes even more complex. What is more, the concepts of a defined group of 'us' and another defined group of 'them' who are 'the other', upon which identity politics and liberation movements have so often built their call and action for justice, is undermined by the understanding of the fragmentation of identity and the fluid notions of power which this analysis brings. 'Others' pro-liferate *ad nauseam* and all call to action dies the death of a thousand qualifica-tions. A new poststructuralist, postmodern feminism poses challenges to the humanist, justice-orientated feminism of the 1960s and 1970s.

I welcome those aspects of a poststructuralist approach which 'define[s] gender as positional, relational, contextual, and political' (Doehring 1999: 101) and also as performed, and accept the benefits which such an emphasis on diversity can bring. Graham instances Mary McClintock Fulkerson's work on the language and subjectivity of poor white women in conservative Pentecostal congregations in the US to show how 'the orthodoxies of liberal feminist theology risk over-riding the experiences of many women' (Graham 1999a: 200; Fulkerson 1994; see also Parsons 2000). Recent exploration of the lives of the mediaeval mystics such as Julian of Norwich, similarly show how practices, including linguistic practices, must be interpreted with fluidity and contextual nuance. It is possible both to live in and with patriarchal practices while pushing at the boundaries from within them (Jantzen 1995a: 158). What is most important, however, is that an appreciation of such subtlety and diversity in the understanding of subjectivity, power and oppression does not undermine the commitment of feminist pastoral theology to its analysis of and fight against the patriarchal structures which prevent the realization of the full humanity of women. That 'humanity' is in itself a fluid concept (certainly not to be identified with the male or any other dominant norm)[16] and that 'womanhood' cannot be universalized, does not necessarily invalidate such analysis and commitment.

16.   See Susan Parsons's critique of Rosemary Radford Ruether (Parsons 2000: 10-13).

Chapter Two

Violence: A Reality in Women's Lives and a Lens for Social and Theological Analysis

This chapter presents two complementary theses. The first is that violence is a pervasive, underlying concrete reality in women's lives. The second is that an examination of the concept of violence provides an interpretative key for pastoral reflection, a lens through which to analyse the patriarchal nature of society and of the church. At the outset it is important to recognize two facts which are also in a different way complementary. Violence against women is global, horrifically extensive and varied, and shaped by gendered understandings and practices. The fact that men also suffer violence on a global scale (which a recent visit to a violence-torn Palestine and Israel has inscribed deeply on my consciousness) must neither be forgotten on the one hand, nor on the other hand allowed in any way to dilute our grasp of the character and reality of violence against women. While both men and women suffer the consequences of violence which has its roots in religious, ethnic, class and sexuality issues, women *in addition* suffer violence by virtue of being women in patriarchal society.

Violence against Women as a Global Reality

When speaking about feminism to groups who might well regard it as a faddish preoccupation of middle-class intellectuals, I often quote from Janet Soskice's use of the economist Amartya Sen's statistics, which demonstrate that 'more than 100 million women are missing':

> it is the persistent failure to give girl children and women medical care similar to that of the men, comparable food and equal access to medical and social provision [which is the important feature]. When there are scarce resources, male children and men get them. Female children and women die in their hundreds of thousands. The title of Sen's article is 'More than 100 Million Women are Missing', because that is the minimum figure by which, if we

projected from male/female ratios in the privileged world, we find a shortfall of women. We are one hundred million women short. Sexism does not simply hurt women's feelings, it kills millions and millions of them (Soskice 1992a: 306).

So the first task is to establish the global nature of violence against women. This violence should be examined not only in its active forms, such as wife-beating, but in its 'passive' forms, such as deprivation of life-giving nourishment and segregated labour markets which accord lower pay and worse conditions to women. 'Of the estimated 1.3 billion people living in poverty world-wide, more than 70 per cent are women and girls' (UNICEF, *State of the World's Children* 1996). It is important to note that this global violence against women arises from understandings and practices which are shaped by gender issues. There are many different causes of violence, some of which are gendered and some of which are not. There are also many different factors at work in the violence and deprivation which women experience; social and economic realities interact with gender factors in a vicious spiral. My concern here is to draw attention to those kinds of violence which occur on a global scale and which have their roots in issues of gender, of the community's understanding of what it means to be a woman and what it means to be a man. The 'persistent failure to give girl children and women' medical care, food and social resources comparable to those given to boys and men indicates a low value placed on the lives of females as opposed to the lives of males.[1]

In 1999 the Journal of the Council for World Mission, *Inside Out*, reported the following interview from the daily *Samoa Observer* newspaper:

Reporter: Do you think domestic violence is a problem in Samoa?
Man: No, it is not really a problem. But why beat your wife? They are useful to do the chores. But if the wife is wrong, she should be beaten, and if she is wrong again, she should be kicked out of the house.
Woman: No, it is not a problem here, if there is love and obedience, then there is good relationship. You must be obedient for a relationship to work. (Quoted in Morton 1999: 8.)

What this conversation highlights is the construction of the man as the 'head of the household' and the way in which such a construction is predicated on the *possibility* of violence. It is salutary to note that Samoa has a virtually 100 per cent Christian population. As will be seen later the construction of male headship is one of the key planks of theologically legitimated violence against women. Sadly such a possibility of violence is all too often realized, and not

---

1.   See Grey (2000b) for a particular study of women in Rajastan, NW India.

only in Samoa. (Adams and Fortune 1995; Mananzan *et al.* 1996). This quotation also demonstrates the attitude to women as servants who are 'useful to do the chores'. Western 'new man' is less likely to use such an expression, at least in mixed company, but the underlying reality of the use of women in society to do domestic chores, take care of the elderly and generally keep the show on the road by doing the less honourable routine tasks at home, at work and in the church, is quite normal in the West. These gendered attitudes (which are often connected with religious legitimation of roles)—of giving a low value to women, of keeping women in compliance through violence, of expecting women to 'do the chores', and of 'honouring' women's work in a patronizing way which serves to keep women in their place—take on specific features which are determined by many different factors, varying according to time and place. Their occurrence in some form is universal.

Sherry Ortner, an anthropologist, refers to the 'universal devaluation of women', and maintains that 'everywhere, in every known culture, women are considered in some degree inferior to men' (Ortner 1995: 38-39). This view is confirmed by the findings of a recent World Council of Churches report. During the Decade of the Churches in Solidarity with Women, launched in 1988, teams from the WCC visited member churches throughout the world. These 'living letters' reported the global feminization of poverty and the universal escalation of violence against women, noting that:

> Although physical violence was the form most openly named and described, we discovered evidence of many types of violence, related and shading into each other—not only physical but also economic, social, structural/institutional, psychological and spiritual (WCC 1997: 23).

So far I have identified as key features in gender-contoured violence a low value given to women, the role of the man as 'head of the family' and the expectation of 'service' from women. A further feature of gender-contoured violence is the maintenance of male control and the exercise of male power, as is illustrated in the following report:

> A 41 year old woman and her 14 year old daughter were murdered on Saturday in Wadi Salame, a Bedouin village near Karmiel [Israel]…many agree that the two were victims of an 'honor killing'. The woman's 21 year old son, Suleiman Suad…was arrested and charged with their deaths… Al-Mithaq reported that the two were targeted because Suleiman felt that 'they were not respecting him as an elder son/brother' (Al-Mithaq, May 4). Other newspapers reported his complaint that his sister spent too much time talking on the telephone as evidence that this was, indeed, an 'honor killing' (HRA International Weekly Press Review 9.5.01).

This horrifying incident highlights the question of control and domination. Keeping women in 'appropriate' submission is an exercise of power which may be used to compensate men for loss of power in other areas of their lives. So, in this particular instance:

> The perpetuation of traditional cultural restrictions placed on Arab women is inextricably linked to the racial oppression of the state and society. Arab men feel powerless under the occupying state and women bear the brunt of this frustration… This general frustration, anger and feelings of impotence has often been cited as contributing to the prevalence of violence against women. This is a cross cultural phenomenon. During the Gulf War when Israel chose not to retaliate under attack from Iraqi missiles, the number of incidences of domestic violence increased dramatically (Bennett Humphries 2000: 18-19).

It is thus quite impossible to examine the violence that women suffer independently of a consideration of the global prevalence of violence in its many forms.

Violence against women happens every day all over the world. It may be perceived or unperceived, named as violence or not seen as a problem, theorized or untheorized. It is my intention to move in the second half of the chapter to explore some theoretical concepts concerning gendered violence which illuminate the nature of society and the problems which need to be addressed. Before doing so I shall first explore the ways in which the church and the Christian tradition are implicated in this gendered violence, and secondly look more deeply into an important aspect of violence against women, which features strongly in religious contexts, that is the connection between violence and silence.

The Complicity of the Church and of the Christian Tradition in Violence against Women

Living Letters documents the complicity of the churches in violence against women. Not only is such violence condoned—'[we] were also struck by many churches' apparent unwillingness to deal effectively with violence. In many places it was said that the church lags behind secular society and the state in awareness and practical action' (WCC 1997: 26)—but it is even given theological justification, for example through the interpretation of biblical man–woman relationships, or the interpretation of certain doctrines of human nature. 'Some men we talked to tried to justify physical violence as a way of helping women "achieve" salvation' (p. 27).

I have seen this phenomenon over and over again in my teaching in Cambridge. In the mid 1990s I taught a course on the theology of Rosemary Radford

Ruether, at the end of which the group (eleven female students, one male student and myself) spent a whole day together writing a liturgy to express what we had learned. Some way into the process a women from the Methodist college said, 'We haven't used the Bible yet. We must have a Bible reading.' A young woman from an Anglican college said, 'I would find that very difficult. The Bible has been used to damage me and downgrade my ministry so often; in this space where I have felt safe I don't want the Bible.' Since this was someone training for ordained ministry, intending to preach regularly from the Bible in her ministry, and currently living and working within a mainstream denominational tradition, I found the incident deeply shocking. It revealed to me the depths of damage which are concealed under 'normal' Christian lives. This incident indicated a use of the Bible to legitimate the dominance of men in the ecclesial and domestic spheres and also to legitimate an estimation of the character, calling and abilities of women, which was experienced as undervaluing to the point of destructiveness.

In an MA seminar group we discussed the interpretation of the texts in the New Testament about wives being submissive to their husbands (Eph. 5.21-33; Col. 3.18-19; 1 Pet. 3.1-6). The group was reluctant to accept that otherwise apparently 'normal' Christian men might deliberately use such texts to justify their own violence against their wives—until one of the members told us that her husband had done so for years. I shall return in much more detail to an examination of the role of the Bible in feminist pastoral theology in Chapter 3. Suffice it to say for the moment that these incidents are in no way isolated, and the connections between a biblical faith and violence are well documented, both in academic research (Fontaine 1997) and in contemporary literature. The father who rules his family by fear in Barbara Kingsolver's *The Poisonwood Bible* (1998) is a typical example.[2]

Violence against women and the devaluing of women are intimately connected. The links between the low value accorded to women and the imaging of God, the Christian teaching on men–women relationships and the construction of Christian community, will be explored further in Chapters 4 and 5. At this stage it is important to recognize that the Christian tradition is riddled with misogynist and consequently violent and devaluing attitudes to women.[3] The following is a striking but by no means isolated example:

2.   As he also tries to dominate the people through language and the land through inappropriate cultivation. This triad of the domination of women, language and land is often found in texts about violence and colonization. I am grateful to Joanne Woolway Grenfell for this insight, see Woolway (1997).

3.   See Loades 1990: Part 2 Christian History and Tradition. For Christian thinking in

In the tenth century Odo of Cluny (died 942) repeated for the benefit of his monks John Chrysostom's warnings against the daughters of Eve: 'Physical beauty is only skin deep. If *men* could see beneath the skin, the sight of *women* would make them nauseous... Since we are loathe to touch spittle or dung even with our fingertips, how can we desire to embrace such a sack of dung?' (Dalarun 1992: 20).

Men are a sack of dung too.

In the tenth century the sentiments of the fourth century are echoed—part of a bridge which stretches in Christian tradition implicitly or explicitly from the creation story and the prophets (see Ezek. 16) through echoes, transformed but not free of ambiguity, in the New Testament (1 Pet. 3.3-5) to the present day. A contemporary example is the provision for alternative episcopal oversight in the Church of England to safeguard those who would otherwise consider themselves 'tainted'—via the laying on of hands—by women's priesthood.[4] Many is the time students have expressed a sense of betrayal that the picture given of Chrysostom, Augustine and other church fathers in typical lectures simply ignores these difficult issues.

There is a consistent feature of the more conservative Christian presentation of the relationship between men and women which centres its self-understanding around the notion of *complementarity*. This is sometimes expressed in terms of men and women having different 'callings' or 'charisms'. Such thinking does not carry the overtly unpleasant and violent overtones of the attitudes illustrated above. It is a common view, widespread in contemporary thinking in Orthodox, Catholic and Evangelical circles and with significant historical roots (Gelder 1996; Martin 1994; Behr-Sigel and Ware 2000). It is, I believe, a pernicious way of thinking. It is superficially attractive because it allows an apparently benign reading of biblical passages which legitimate male headship, it gives a theoretical account of why women may not be allowed certain roles, such as ordination, without explicitly suggesting women's inferiority, and it makes sense of the *de facto* situation that certain roles are taken by women and certain by men for either biological or cultural reasons. Indeed it gives religious legitimation to such roles. This is the key to the pernicious nature of 'complementarity'.

The idea of the complementarity of the sexes as popularly propounded in many Christian circles is ideologically naive. 'The ideology of complementarity

context of wider secular views see O'Faolain and Martines, *Not in God's Image* (1979; collection of quotations) or for more detailed essays Duby and Perrot, *A History of Women in the West* (1992). The assumptions made about women by the characters in Eco's *The Name of the Rose* illustrate the point strikingly with respect to the mediaeval period.

4.   'The Act of Synod is patriarchy unmasked. It represents the wholly unacceptable concept that women are objects of taint and abnormality' (Thorne 2000: 124).

masks the reality of dependence' (Ruether 1989: 106). Indeed, the rhetoric of complementarity often masks the reality of domination and power abuse. The feminist theorist Catherine MacKinnon makes the point graphically: 'Difference is the velvet glove on the iron fist of domination' (1989: 218-19). MacKinnon's thesis concerning gender, difference and power will be examined in more detail below; the key point here is that complementarity, or the enshrining of gender differences into a legitimated pattern of roles and relationships, is not as innocent as at first sight. It may lead to explicit exclusion of one side of the 'complementarity' from privileges, esteem or practical roles. The question must then be asked—who has the power to do this excluding? Who is creating and inscribing these differences with these excluding outcomes? While many Christian women themselves espouse the notion and practices of complementarity, the fact must be faced that it is men, not women, who have constructed this religious perspective, in biblical writing and authoritative teaching tradition. As the oppressed may, and often do, internalize their oppression and imbibe its values, the fact that women espouse this male-constructed perspective and practice is no guarantee of its appropriateness for women. There is a dilemma for feminist theology here, as the commitment to hear and value women's own stories and voices is held in tension with an understanding of the psychological and social processes of the internalization of ideological oppression. These issues are not easily resolved, but that complementarity is at the very least an ambiguous notion seems indisputable. It must be considered in any exploration of the church's complicity in violence against women. There may seem to be huge steps from 'women are more suited for different roles under God' to 'keeping women in submission' to 'violence against women', but I propose that there is a direct connection in principle, which becomes a route all too often travelled in practice.

Violence and Silence

In Chapter 1 I raised the question of women's silencing in the context of feminist research and writing. Silencing is intimately connected with violence—implicit and explicit. In further development of the theme of violence as a pervasive, underlying concrete reality in women's lives I would instance the following aspects of women's silence: the conspiracy of silence, fear of speaking out against abuse, the 'unstory' in the face of the dominant sociocultural narrative, epistemological silence, silence in women's spirituality and the reduction to silence in moral argument. These 'silences' are all manifested within church contexts as well as wider social contexts.

The expression 'conspiracy of silence' is normally used to indicate the cover-up of a specific issue or abuse. It seems to me an appropriate expression for the whole phenomenon of the refusal to name women's problems (Friedan 1963—'the problem with no name'), for the incredibility of women when they do attempt to tell their stories (Bons-Storm 1996) and for the way in which women's analysis of society as patriarchal, and their commitment to change it, is so often cast as 'strident', extremist and marginal. So many women's problems are ones nobody else really wants to know about. Mary Grey writes of 'moving beyond the silence' in rural Rajasthan (India) where extreme poverty hits women hardest but in which the outside world is not interested—'Disaster prevention is not newsworthy' (Grey 2000b: 34). In a quite different context a clergyman recently said to me that it was important to have a respected senior woman in the diocese to deal with (slightly hushed voice) 'women's problems'. For a confused moment I thought he was referring to gynaecological or menstrual problems, until I realized he meant opposition to women's priesthood. The conspiracy of silence has a thousand faces.

This general conspiracy is illustrated particularly in the issue of sexually related abuse. Domestic violence has only been named and known as such in a widespread way since the 1970s, and the interview from Samoa above indicates that it is not so known and named everywhere. Indeed it is only since 1990 that British law has recognized marital rape. This and other forms of sexual abuse are constantly covered up, and one of the ways of covering up is to refuse to describe and name. Peter Rutter, in his research on abuse of women by men in power—therapists, doctors, clergy, teachers—describes how finding a name for the phenomenon he wanted to research and make public was so important:

> In order to break through the complex psychological and cultural curtain of silence protecting men in power who abuse women's trust, the syndrome had to be named in its broadest context. [He calls it 'sex in the forbidden zone'.] Our attempts to understand the darker corners of the human condition are significantly impeded when we lack a vocabulary with which to name the damaging ways people treat one another… Identifying a mode of behaviour by giving it a name with negative connotations is one of the earliest signs that some members of a society are beginning to challenge the acceptability of that behaviour… Even the term *sexual harrassment* began to be used in its current meaning only as recently as 1976. One can imagine women in the workplace before then searching to describe how they were being treated, trying to find a way to express the feeling that they no longer wanted to accept this treatment as 'normal' (Rutter 1989: 23).

Rutter shows well both the importance of naming, and also how that naming is part of refusing the conspiracy of silence which takes such abuse as unimportant or even refuses to admit that it happens. It is to me significant that Rutter's book was sent to me as a great discovery by a close friend, in a mutual attempt to understand different but related experiences of sexually inappropriate behaviour by clergy towards us. My copy has since been read by countless other women as they began to understand and name their own similar experiences.

It is not only in relation to explicit sexual abuse that this issue of silence is important. Finding a name to express feelings and even to identify events and actions is an essential part of being able to convey these feelings and events in a meaningful way in the outside world. Concerning the 'unstory' or inability of women to tell their own story credibly (Bons-Storm 1996) the key point in relation to violence is that the dominant narrative is held in place by structures of power and control. These are institutional, linguistic, economic, intellectual and religious. Women are frequently required not only to justify their stories in a male-dominated institution, but also to express them in the language and thought-forms of male-dominated philosophical, psychological and religious traditions. As Bons-Storm says:

> The roles women are allowed to play, according to the dominant socio-cultural narrative…restrict women to a narrow space in which they can develop their identity and self-narrative. Outside this narrow space they enter the vast territory of shame and guilt feelings, mixed with rebellious feelings of an emerging and developing subject quality (1996: 134-35).

When such a situation is maintained, that maintenance of itself implies violence. It is not necessarily actualized violence; it is not necessarily physical violence (though it may be either or both). It is implicit, often internalized violence. It is insidious pressure. Its results are manifested in ways which may be hidden until exposed. The great value of Bons-Storm's book is that she gives this problem exposure in the context of pastoral care and counselling.

In a wider epistemological context Belenky *et al.* (1986) in their influential study of 'women's ways of knowing' identify how these may be submerged and not accorded high value in the public domain. Particularly interesting here is their investigation of the level of 'knowing' which is in fact silence, an inability self-consciously to articulate any knowledge at all. This silence is in many cases empirically connected with experiences of violence (verbal or physical) in childhood. To speak and articulate knowledge is to risk a verbal or physical lashing. Moreover, words have only been experienced by many women as means of inflicting violence, so no positive role for verbal communication is known.

These findings and this analysis are complemented by those of Nicola Slee in her work on women's spirituality. She describes what she calls an 'apophatic faith stance' in which women's attempts to describe faith experience positively:

> were full of qualifiers, contradictions, pauses, stumblings and a curious, rather flat use of stock terms and phrases, all of which gave an impression of distance from experience and a kind of obfuscating layer between the experience and her own assimilation of it (2001: 27).

Slee identifies positive features in this faith stance and in some aspects of its expression, but, significantly in this context, one of the categories of women who experience this reduction to silence or stumbling speech is those 'women who had experienced religion as a predominantly negative and oppressive force in their lives' (2001: 28).

Finally, the work of Carol Gilligan on women's moral development points to the way in which our understanding of normative moral development has been based on research among men, in such a way as to make the 'different voice', often that of girls and women, seem less adequate. Research is so conducted and the terms of discussion so set up, that the typically female voice is reduced to silence and confusion. In the examination of a moral dilemma in which a boy's and a girl's construal are compared, 'Amy's confidence begins to diminish, and her replies become more constrained and unsure' (Gilligan 1993: 29). The issue for my argument is not so much one of the substance of any possible differences between male and female psychological development, but the way in which the dominant narrative inscribes male experience and moral reasoning as normative, reducing to silence female experience and moral reasoning, and constructing these as having less value, and thus less power in society. Gilligan raised these questions:

> not as abstract philosophical speculations about the nature of reality and truth but as personal doubts that invade women's sense of themselves, compromising their ability to act on their own perceptions and thus their willingness to take responsibility for what they do (1993: 49).

I have sought to show that violence is a pervasive, underlying concrete reality in women's lives. Such violence is found in the global feminization of poverty, in physical domestic violence even to the point of the killing of women, in religiously motivated control and chastisement, in violent and sexually abusive language, in the refusal of certain roles to women and the exclusion of them from decision-making, in ideological claims by men to construct what it means to be a women, in sexual abuse and harassment, and in the pressure to remain silent in the face of this. Similarly violence is found in the exclusion of women from the construction of knowledge (Code 1991) and

women find it much more difficult to object to things in public domain: feel guilty at doing it

[handwritten margin note top: Is it, or is it just women that are at home so not writing papers.]

the dominant discourses of philosophy, of psychology, of religion, and of morality. All of this is violence, whether explicit or implicit. It touches all spheres of life and prevails globally.

Violence as a Lens for Social and Theological Analysis

This de facto situation, that women live to a greater or lesser extent under the reality or the threat of violence, provides a fruitful lens through which to theorize and thus expose the patriarchal nature of society and of the church. There are four key elements to this analysis of patriarchy. First, the maintenance of inequality implies violence; therefore patriarchy implies violence. Second, the complex symbolic representations of sexual difference are mapped on to economic and social inequality, thus rendering it an instrument for the maintenance of inequality by violence. Third, male dominance is sexualized and thrives on the objectification and abuse of women. Fourth, 'we have focused the conditions for violence in the heart of the male role and male identity' (Pellauer 1985: 49).

Patriarchy Implies Violence

I have already indicated the sense in which the maintenance of a state of inequality implies the necessary force (or violence) to keep that state of affairs intact. Political dictatorships, colonialism and the maintenance of the apartheid regime in South Africa are clear examples. Attempts to maintain the control of children by parents or school teachers furnish more ambiguous examples, as it would be normally agreed both that such control has benign and useful elements but also that such control is often abused in a way that has explicitly violent physical and psychological features. Any evaluative interpretation of these examples of the maintenance of inequality will depend on contextual factors and on underlying values and perspectives. The maintenance of inequality, or indeed of 'complementarity', between men and women may have features, or be understood as having features, of either or both of these types of control, and will be variously evaluated. My point is simply that the maintenance of inequality implies a control which is intimately connected with violence and force. This 'violence' may be evaluated negatively by some only when it becomes 'excessive'; for others the very necessity to 'maintain' a state of affairs implies an unacceptable underlying violence.

[handwritten margin note left: Use these 2 factors in assessing marital issues]

The similarity of the words 'violence' and 'violation' is significant. The violence of a patriarchal system manifests itself in the violation of women's bodies, for example in domestic violence, in military rape, or in reproductive control. It is manifested in the violation of the natural world. A key feature of recent feminist discussion is the acknowledgment of the interlocking nature of various forms of violence (Mananzan *et al.* 1996). A feminism that does not take account of the oppressions of class and race is a truncated feminism. It is truncated because the actual historical conditions under which women live are structured by economic, class, racial and ethnic factors which articulate in various ways with gendered factors. Therefore only a very partial social analysis can be made from one perspective alone. It is also truncated because the commitment to justice that fires the feminist cause becomes merely a commitment to getting the best for one particular group if it does not embrace those beyond its own agenda. To this must be added an understanding of the connections between ecological concerns and human social justice, and a commitment to sustain the integrity of the non-human world.

It is crucial to realize that this is not a discussion about whether women are as capable of being violent as men. It is clear that women can show great violence. It is also clear that the purity of 'sisterhood' is a myth (West 1995). The question is whether violence, and consequently violation, is an inevitable concomitant (both logically and empirically) of the global maintenance of a patriarchal system.[5]

Sexual Difference: Symbolic Difference Mapped onto Economic and Social Inequality
Binary oppositions have a tenacious hold in most Western traditions of thinking, and they often serve to hold in place symbolic contrasts and differences. I mentioned above the connections between the violation of women and the violation of nature. Women have been seen almost universally as closer to 'nature' than men, who are identified with 'culture', normally regarded as superior to nature, transcending nature (Ortner 1995). Symbolic connections are made between women and nature (earth mother), some of which cluster around the language of violation (the rape of the earth). In this linguistic transaction values and qualities are carried across from one party to the other. This particular 'mapping' of the qualities of nature onto the qualities of women serves to allow the identification of men with culture (constructed as the binary opposite of nature), taking the central roles in politics, commerce, higher education, the construction of knowledge, law, artistic endeavour and public life in general.

Christian thinking has inherited both a tradition of the disgust at female sexuality (as indicated in the more lurid comparisons of the unfaithfulness of Israel with female sexual promiscuity in Ezekiel and Hosea) and also a Greek philosophical tradition of binary oppositions such as light and dark, soul and

5.   'All known societies are patriarchal' (Giddens 1989: 199).

body. The soul, or rational faculty, has been exalted above the body ('nature', 'dark', 'sexually uncontrolled'). When this binary opposition is mapped on to sexual difference, in the context of a negative view of female sexuality, a particularly potent brew is concocted. Women come to be identified with the bodily or non-rational element of human nature (as will be seen further in discussion of the *imago dei* doctrine) and female sexuality is identified as a source of evil and temptation. This can be seen in a range of views, practices and symbols down the centuries, from the exaltation of the spotless virginity of Mary to the destruction of the real human flesh of poor women accused of witchcraft. An excerpt from the 'Hammer of Witches', written at the time of the hunting and burning of women as witches, illustrates the point:

> Since they [women] are weak, they find an easy and secret manner of vindicating themselves in witchcraft. They are feebler both in mind and body. It is not surprising they should come under the spell of witchcraft. As regards intellect or understanding of spiritual things, they seem to be of a different nature than men… Women are intellectually like children…always more prone to abjure the faith… [having] inordinate passions… (*Malleus Maleficarum* 1486).

It is impossible, in an analysis of patriarchy, to separate out the symbolic from the material realities of life, as this example shows clearly. Symbol and social condition go together (Ruether 1975). The violence done to women in the witch-hunts of the Middle Ages and later (thousands if not millions tortured and burned alive[6]) had root causes in the material factors of the social unrest of the times and the violent abuse of power by the church. It is, however, incomprehensible without the accompanying symbolism of woman as the emotionally weak, sexually depraved descendent of Eve, who succumbed to the devil. An example nearer our own time illustrates the same point. Why, asks Kate Figes (*Because of Her Sex* 1994) in spite of years of equal opportunities legislation in the workplace in Britain, is the labour market still segregated, with women on lower pay in less desirable jobs? She attempts to answer the question in terms of economics, ignoring such issues as inclusive language and private relationships. It is my contention that such an approach is doomed to failure, since the symbolic and the 'private' are integrally related to the economic and the public. An equal opportunities analysis will never penetrate to the depths of a feminist analysis, since it fails to take account of the depth of the structures of violence inherent in patriarchy which produce the ways in which the female sex is regarded and treated, and the value which is accorded women.

6.   Estimates vary, but the figure of about 1 million is often quoted (see Ruether 1975: 89).

To say that a material, economic analysis alone is insufficient is not to say that the material, social, economic factors are unimportant. Far from it. I believe there is much to be learned, especially in the church, from Catherine MacKinnon's argument that sexual difference would not hold such a high place in our consciousness if it were not that sexual difference is mapped on to economic and social inequality. As she says, 'Gender might not even code as difference, might not mean distinction epistemologically, were it not for its consequences for social power (MacKinnon 1989: 219). MacKinnon's thesis, from the perspective of law and the theory of the state, is that material inequalities and inequalities of power are the primary data; explication and legitimation of these in terms of differences between the sexes come second. 'Differences are inequality's *post hoc* excuse' (p. 218). Her argument is based on the assertion that inequality is a material condition whereas 'difference' is an idea. Inevitably there is a certain circularity here concerning whether ideas lead to practice or practices lead to ideas which support and legitimate them. Both are the case; indeed this is a potentially vicious circle. Viewed from this perspective the apparently 'benign' religious assertions of difference and complementarity between the sexes, especially where these serve to exclude women from power, take on a more sinister aspect.

In sum, it is of the utmost importance to analyse both material conditions *and* their ideological underpinning in terms of language, ideas and symbolism, and also to excavate the layers of mapping, as sets of patriarchal symbols and sets of patriarchal practices become stronger by mutual reinforcement. As an anecdotal but telling rider to this discussion I would add that I find it hard to believe I will ever have deep material or symbolic equality as a woman in a society where I can go into a shop with a friend to collect two rucksacks and be told—'Ah, yes, I have them put by here—one ladies' and one normal'.

Sexualized Male Dominance and the Objectification of Women

Pornography and rape are two issues which have been extensively analysed by feminist writers in such a way as to bring out important features of the patriarchal structure of society. These features are as follows. Power and control exercised by men over women are intimately connected with sex and the use of sex; a feature of this use of sex as a controlling mechanism is the objectification of women; sexual dominance and objectification structure women's lives even when specific instances of identified violent behaviour are not currently experienced.

Radical feminists have waged a consistent war against pornography, despite the gradual winning of women as an audience for pornography from the 1980s

(Jeffreys 1992: 470). This war is fuelled by the belief that there is a demonstrable link between a range of inequalities in society, an ideology of male sexual domination, and sexual violence against women. This ideology 'posits that men are superior to women by virtue of their penises…that the sexual will of men properly and naturally defines the parameters of a woman's sexual being, which is her whole identity' (Dworkin 1981: 203). Furthermore it pervades the whole social sphere since, 'With the rape and prostitution in which it participates, pornography institutionalizes the sexuality of male supremacy, which fuses the eroticization of dominance and submission with the social construction of male and female. Gender is sexual' (MacKinnon 1984: 326).

This radical feminist view of pornography (well summarised in Jeffreys 1992), even though it needs further refinement in the light of a postmodern understanding of the complexities of power and meaning, does make clear the important role of male sexual identity in an analysis of violence. Rape and prostitution in war further underline these connections, as does an analysis of the way military ideology is constructed. As Susan Brookes Thistlethwaite explains, 'sexuality and relationships…get constructed as violence, as the chant taught at many US boot camps attests: "This is my weapon, this is my gun, One is for shooting, the other's for fun"' (1996: 121). This linking of the penis, the gun and the male role and identity is all the more sinister in a Christian context given the way similar symbolism can be used. Elisabeth Behr-Sigel quotes Paul Evdokimov '"Man the witness" acts through his virile energy; by means of his priestly powers he pierces the flesh of this world. He is the "violent one", of which the gospel speaks (Matt. 11.12)' (quoted in Behr-Sigel and Ware 2000: 18).

The 'objectification' of women plays a significant role in the prevalence of male sexual violence. Objectification is a process whereby a more powerful group defines a less powerful group as objects or tools, less than fully human. Rosemary Radford Ruether (1975) gives what she calls a historical account, a social analysis and a psychological archaeology which traces a line from the use of women as objects and tools, through the denigration of women, stemming from paranoia and fear of women's bodies as sources of temptation and repositories of evil, through to the idealization of women. All these modes are male constructions of women, seen through the dominant and sexualized gaze of men and represented by men in the dominant sociocultural narrative. 'Woman' is constructed as 'other', as object not subject. As such women are vulnerable to being 'used'.

Susan Brownmiller's understanding of rape as part of a system of male intimidation which keeps all women in fear, further illuminates the way in which male violence structures women's lives (Brownmiller 1975). This has two aspects. Any of the millions of lists of 'dos and don'ts' issued to women concerning their own protection speaks eloquently of the way in which women's whole lives—from going out socially, to whose voice is on the answerphone, to how and where travel is possible—is structured by the need for self-protection against male sexual violence. But the question must be asked whether these measures against the possible attack from a stranger, probably thought of as a pervert or at least an exception, really hit the main problem, since 'rape is not the act of a sex-driven individual against a stranger but a relatively common act, usually between people who know each other' (Lockley 1999: 5). This is seen in date-rape, incest and partner domestic violence.

The second aspect of this wide understanding of the significance of rape and the threat and fear of rape is the importance of recognizing that rape is an inevitable consequence of a society in which male power, violence and sexuality are valued in the way they are. To isolate the rapist as a 'sick individual' is to ignore the fundamental way in which his behaviour is connected to the whole social system. The rapist should not be seen as 'an extreme individual'. The statistics show that 'rapists are common in society and associated with male gender dominated beliefs. Moreover, rapists are likely to have a macho personality, endorse callous sex attitudes towards women, and see violence as manly' (Lockley 1999: 4). The practices that involve the representation and the acting out of violence from men towards women, as can be seen in both pornography and rape, are deeply implicated in the general attitudes of a patriarchal society and cannot be isolated as 'sick'. The possibility, indeed the inevitability, of such outworkings of male dominance over women are already given in the construction and acceptance of a patriarchal society.

'We have Focused the Conditions for Violence in the Heart of the Male Role and Male Identity'

Pellauer (1985: 49) writes of the 'moral callousness' which many people have built up—of the thick skin which protects us from feeling and pain. But ultimately these 'calluses' *alienate* people from their own feeling and pain, allowing them to inflict pain on others without feeling it. In a society in which boys may not cry and men may not acknowledge weakness and vulnerability, we should not be surprised if we often look in vain for sensitivity to the pain of women. Only last weekend I overheard the stub end of a conversation on the underground train: man to woman, obviously about his son who lived with his estranged partner, 'I don't want him to grow up too namby-pamby; he spends so much time with his mother'. 'Hardness' is a recognized male quality. It is not only feminists who pay attention to the construction of the male role as hard and even violent, and to the damage that this does. James Poling writes in *The Care of Men*:

> How can violent men, many of whom are Christians, engage in violence against women and children and not seek help from pastors and other caregivers? Because the churches have not identified male violence as a pressing ethical and religious issue. Why do many churches refuse to see male violence as a major threat to the health of women, children, and families and instead call for a return to 'family values' (the male-dominated, heterosexual nuclear family) as a solution to society's ills? Because the church's patriarchal theology gives priority to the rights of men over women and children (Neuger and Poling 1997: 139).

Recently a burgeoning theology of masculinity is seeking to address these issues, taking on board the feminist critique of patriarchy (Neuger and Poling 1997; Pryce 1996). In seeking to encourage the transformation and flourishing of a community built on love, which is the ultimate aim of feminist pastoral theology, we must, as feminists, work together with men who share the same goal and the same understanding of the patriarchal nature of society, to free men as well as women from the violence of the role we have constructed for men in the church just as much, or even more, than in society.

Postscript on Method

I have placed the chapter on violence at the beginning of this study because it is the seriousness of the issues raised here that is the spur to my contention that feminist theology is not an optional extra but is demanded by the very nature of the gospel, which calls for the practices of love and justice from its adherents. I have also placed it here for a methodological reason. The chapters that follow are an attempt to re-examine some central practices and beliefs of the Christian tradition. These involve theological issues such as the nature of God, the person of Jesus Christ, what it means to be a human being in the world today and in the ultimate loving purposes of God, and what it might mean to speak of the revelation of God's truth to us. They also concern matters of how Christian communities live out and preach their beliefs, and give and receive pastoral care. Violence will be the lens through which I examine all this. That lens has, as in this chapter, two foci—the reality of violence, explicit or implicit, physical or emotional, in women's lives; and the interpretative key of violence, which opens up an understanding of the historical condition of patriarchy under which we all live.

Elie Wiesel, in writing about the holocaust, memorably said that whatever theology we espouse we must be able to hold it in the presence of burning babies. Likewise we must be able to hold our theology in the presence of those 100 million women who are missing, and of the eight-year-old Asian girls who are wakened nightly in their rooms to attend to the demands of sex tourists. It will not do to say that these are the aberrant actions of sick individuals: 'no man [or woman] is an island' and gendered violence is of the essence of our world. This is the context in which pastoral theology must be thought and lived.

Chapter Three

The Bible: The 'Master's Tool' or 'Flashes of Alternative Possibilities'

Gendered violence is frightening and sickening. The connections between gendered violence, Christian texts and the Christian churches *must* be faced head on. For those like myself, brought up in Evangelical or traditional Christian environments, the suggestion that the Bible, the Word of God, has played a part in fostering violent and destructive behaviour is deeply disturbing. But we do neither the cause of truth nor the cause of justice any favours by refusing the difficulties. For some readers of this book the 'authority of God's Word' has been experienced as a source of nourishment and as a challenge to right action. For others it has been experienced as painful oppression or as an excuse for cruel action. Is there any way in which the two perspectives, the two sets of vital questions, may at least be held in tension, if not reconciled? There are those who take the feminist critique seriously who have come to reject any recognizable 'authority of Scripture'. Others radically reinterpret the meaning of 'authority' in ways which still allow for a special place for the Bible within the Christian community, and for fruitful interaction with it. Yet others wrestle to retain a traditionally conservative stance with regard to the Bible and its authority while taking seriously the issues raised in Chapter 2.[1]

Audre Lourde famously said that 'the master's tools will never dismantle the master's house'. There is no doubt that the Bible has been used and abused by 'masters' to use and abuse women and that only a radically new set of tools will dismantle the house of patriarchal religion. But that is not to say that the Bible is itself in this sense a 'master's tool'. Certainly it is not *only* a master's

---

1. I supervise an increasing number of undergraduate and postgraduate dissertations in the University of Cambridge and in the Cambridge Theological Federation in which young women from Evangelical traditions seek to explore with impressive existential, spiritual and intellectual vigour the feminist and the Evangelical/scriptural perpectives and to come to a place where they can reconcile these perspectives.

tool; it is much more than this. Within that record of and witness to the faith of so many people through the ages, may be found the record of and witness to the love of God for humanity and for all creation. Within the Bible are 'flashes of alternative possibilities' (Hampson and Ruether 1987: 19)—shining glimpses of new and bright hope, radical and disturbing suggestions of the ways of justice and the paths of peace.

Why is it Important to Consider the Bible in Feminist Pastoral Theology?

The Bible is indeed a double-edged sword. It is and has been both the source of women's subordination and suffering and also the source of women's power and emancipation. Even those who are sceptical about the power of the Bible for good must turn their attention to it as part of the struggle within Christian communities (and the secular communities they help to shape) for women's emancipation. This was the position of Elizabeth Cady Stanton, who in 1885 published the *Woman's Bible*, an attempt to expurgate those elements of Scripture's teaching which are negative about women, and to claim biblical interpretation for women:

> Over and against those who saw the project as a waste of time, Cady Stanton insisted on its political necessity. She argued that it is important for women to interpret the Bible, because scripture and its authority have been and continue to be used against women struggling for emancipation. Moreover, women as well as men have internalized scripture's misogynist teachings as the Word of God (Schüssler Fiorenza 1994: 1).

Cady Stanton saw (white) women's political and social degradation in nineteenth-century America as 'but an outgrowth of [their] status in the Bible' (Stanton 1993: 10). The thrust of her quest was for liberation *in spite of* the Bible.

But this is not the only way in which the Bible has functioned for women. In a quite different sociohistorical context, feminist biblical interpretation in late twentieth-century Africa, Teresa Okure has written:

> the quest for liberation through the Bible in Africa is not a special preserve of women. Men and the poor also have recourse to the same book and believe firmly in it… Africans see the 'word' of God as being most capable of fulfilling what it promises… It therefore becomes most necessary to ensure a correct understanding of this word so as to be firmly committed to its liberative truth: the full liberation of women and men in, and by, and through Jesus Christ (John 8.31-36). Feminist hermeneutics is a reliable tool for achieving this (Okure 1993: 83).

Not only does the Bible function quite differently in different sociohistorical situations, but interpretation and appropriation of the Bible also depend on the theological beliefs that underpin the interpretative stance, and on the personal and communal history and perspective of the interpreter. What is clear from the range of feminist interpretative models currently on offer is that the Bible has *potential* for both the oppression and the liberation of women.[2]

I have always begun my own teaching on feminist pastoral theology with detailed attention to feminist biblical interpretation. My original reason for this was historical. Biblical studies was the first major area to receive widespread attention from feminist theologians.[3] What has become abundantly clear in the course of several years' teaching is that for students from a whole variety of widely different Christian backgrounds this is an excellent place to start. Cherished beliefs, unexamined assumptions, nagging problems, whole lives of identity formation are brought out and drawn into dialogue with a new (for some radically new) feminist perspective on the Bible. The Bible has been, explicitly or implicitly, the base text forming and informing religious identity and understanding of God. Tackling it head on is a critical moment in pastoral theology.

The first piece of work in the course involves commenting on a short biblical passage of the student's choice. There was a problem even in how to describe this (not being able to find a word for something is reminiscent of the operation of 'silence' as explored in the previous chapter, and is also an indication of entering uncharted waters). At first I referred to the work as an 'exegesis', but fell foul of constant anxiety on the part of the students that what I was asking them to do was nothing like exegesis as required on other courses. So I tried 'commentary', but that implied a genre with which many feminists have serious problems, suggesting as it often does a certain claim to comprehensive treatment, and an intention to survey the works of others in secondary fashion. Now I ask for 'comments' from a feminist perspective. The object of the exercise is not only to promote an understanding of various feminist hermeneutical approaches, but to invite creative engagement with a passage of

---

2.   An instructive selection of the range of current approaches in practice can be seen by comparing the following books: Carol A. Newsom and Sharon H. Ringe, *The Women's Bible Commentary* (1992); Elizabeth Schüssler Fiorenza (ed.), *Searching the Scriptures* (1993b; 1994); Catherine Clark Kroeger, Mary Evans and Elaine Storkey (eds.), *The Women's Study New Testament* (1995); the Feminist Companion Series, including Athalya Brenner and Carol Fontaine (eds.), *A Feminist Companion to Reading the Bible* (1997).

3.   *JSOT* 22 (1982) has several important essays on 'The Effects of Women's Studies on Biblical Studies'.

Scripture, giving permission for the imagination to flow freely. Among the wide range of strategies used and issues addressed the following recur regularly and illustrate the importance of the Bible to feminist pastoral theology.

First there are those many students from Evangelical backgrounds who need to wrestle with the key question of authority. How, if at all, is the feminist commitment to the priority of women's experience to be understood in connection with a commitment to live under the authority of the text? Surely it is *men's interpretation of the text* which has been damaging to women, not the real meaning of the text itself? Work is done on what a specific text might have to offer positively in the light of the feminist critique. This wrestling normally leads to a reinterpretation and renewed understanding not only of specific texts but of the text as a whole and of what it means to have a canonical text.

Then there are those whose primary drive is to face up to the 'texts of terror' (Trible 1984). They use passages of the Bible that include violent stories and language concerning women, such as the rape of Tamar, or one of the prophetic passages which speak of women's sexuality in graphically foul terms and of God in shockingly violent language (Hos. 2; Ezek. 16). This is about looking and listening, about noticing what has previously been glossed over, about seeing the Bible in a new light. It is about *not refusing* the ambiguous, the terrifying and the disgusting; and it is about *refusing* to sanitize the Bible in the interests of human or divine respectability.

Many, especially women, choose to explore passages in the Bible about women—Mary in the Magnificat, the woman looking for lost coins, Deborah, the wise women in Proverbs. The Bible is a religiously powerful text, which shapes the identity and intentional living of Christians. It is not surprising therefore that women seek to find themselves in the text, to identify themselves in 'God's story'. Another slightly more adventurous version of this 'finding oneself in the text' is to create an imaginative reconstruction of a text, inserting women or women's thought and speech, into it. Examples have been: reading the story of Jesus' appearing on the road to Emmaus (Lk. 24) with one of the disciples as a woman, exploring the thoughts of the woman taken in adultery (Jn 8), giving a voice to the woman who anointed Jesus' feet (Lk. 7). A striking example of this kind of reconstruction in which we insert ourselves into the text, however obliquely, occurred some years ago in the first feminist theology course I ever taught—in which the participants were four men. At the end of the course we wrote together, as part of the assessment, a creative story based on the invitation to the great banquet (Lk. 14). It was only afterwards that we realized we had written about four men and one woman (Bennett Moore: 1998b)!

Key Issues in Feminist Interpretation of the Bible

The history of women's intellectual and spiritual interpretation and appropriation of the Bible is not confined to self-consciously feminist hermeneutics.
'How', asks Elisabeth Gössmann, 'did Christian women read the Bible in the
centuries that preceded modern feminist interpretation?' She reads the theological works of European women from the Middle Ages to the early modern era to
unearth the biblical interpretation that underlies their work (Gössmann 1993:
27). The feminist commentary *Searching the Scriptures* celebrates the pioneering
work in nineteenth-century America of Elizabeth Cady Stanton, and of Anna
Julia Cooper, a Black feminist, social reformer and interpreter of Scripture
(Schüssler Fiorenza 1993b; Baker-Fletcher 1993). It is, however, with 'second
wave' feminism, and the self-consciously 'feminist' approach to biblical interpretation that I am most concerned. Since the 1980s feminist works on biblical
interpretation have appeared in abundance, as have attempts to offer typologies
of the various feminist strategies of interpretation. I do not propose to offer
either a comprehensive history or my own typology.[4] I propose rather to select
certain approaches which are of direct relevance for feminist pastoral theology.

Rejection of the Bible
The British feminist theologian Daphne Hampson rejects the Bible, along
with Christianity as a whole, as irredeemably sexist. Christianity is set in a
concrete history, is presented in a core symbolism, and is wedded to a foundational narrative, all of which are deeply and irrevocably patriarchal. 'Biblical
stories, and the narration of history in the bible, may be profoundly damaging
to human relations' (Hampson 1990: 87).

This is a most important point for pastoral theology. Even if we reject
Hampson's rejection of Christianity as a whole—which, incidentally, is not
itself based on the incompatibility of feminism and Christianity but on other
arguments (1990: 41)—we cannot ignore the force of her assertion that patriarchal Christianity has damaged human relationships, and in particular relationships between men and women. Christian 'values' based on Christian
texts and Christian symbolism are behind much of the violence and suffering
experienced by women, as shown in Chapter 2. Hampson claims that 'the
text is a product of a sexist, indeed misogynist, culture: the presuppositions of

---

4.   For access to such material, and for further bibliography, the reader is referred in the
first instance to the articles 'The Bible as a Resource for Women' and 'Biblical Exegesis' in
Isherwood and McEwan (1996); 'Biblical Criticism' and 'Biblical Studies' in Russell and
Clarkson (1996).

a patriarchal world are written into it. Moreover, such texts are the more dangerous in that they affect us at a subconscious level' (1990: 92).

Because the biblical texts are sacred texts and because Christianity is a religion of revelation in history then this pernicious influence on the health of human relationships is, according to Hampson, only to be avoided by the wholesale rejection of the Bible and, with it, Christianity. Christianity as a religion is *in its essence* biased against women, and for women to fight for real equality within it is both demeaning and doomed to defeat.

This is a most serious charge, with prima facie credibility. Hampson puts the case succinctly and powerfully. A pastoral theology that is committed to the flourishing of both men and women in community must engage with the Bible in the light of this critique. It is my view that no mileage is to be gained by attempting to answer this charge by means of detailed textual exegesis. It may well be that certain texts (e.g. Gen. 3 and 1 Cor. 11) have been misinterpreted, and, if so, such misinterpretation should indeed be exposed. However, Hampson's charge goes deeper than this. It is that the Bible was written in a patriarchal culture, and so the overall thrust of the ethos it portrays, and invites the reader and the believer to share, is patriarchal (or at the very least contain substantial patriarchal elements). It is within this context and against this issue that whatever strategies of feminist interpretation the pastoral theologian would use must be worked out and tested.

A Liberationist Approach

In a debate with Daphne Hampson in London in 1986, Rosemary Radford Ruether challenged Hampson's thesis on the basis that it was grounded on an inadequate understanding of the meaning of history. Asking 'is there a place for feminists in a Christian church?', Ruether argued that Christianity is not, as Hampson asserts, a historical religion in the sense of being 'enclosed in a past revelation'; rather, she suggested, it is 'an eschatological faith. It lives by the norm of the reign of God in the still unrealized future of creation, not by a fixed, completed past' (1987: 15).

The emphases here on eschatology, on the reign of God as the yet unrealized future, and implicitly on the hope for creation and the need to work for this future with God in faith, are all characteristic of the liberationist approach to theology which has inspired Ruether's lifelong work. This is a key element in much early feminist biblical interpretation (Russell 1985) and continues to resonate as a central theme globally.

A liberationist hermeneutic of Scripture interprets the Bible in the light of God's love and concern for the least in society. It is sometimes said of this approach that it puts human experience 'above' Scripture (whether that be the experience of the poor in general, or the experience of women in particular). This criticism misses the mark. The situation is more complex. God's love for the least, God's call to radical justice and to human community where all are accorded equal worth, are in themselves seen to be the core of the gospel and the imperative of the gospel *precisely as witnessed in the Scriptures*. The Bible as a whole is seen to reflect a mixed bag of ideological commitments concerning religion, theology, society and ethics. From a feminist perspective it is possible, on this understanding of Scripture, to find a fundamentally positive, albeit seriously critical, engagement with the Scriptures.

Ruether refers to this as the principle of *correlation* (Ruether 1985c). Feminist theology is committed on principle to the critique of patriarchy as ideological oppression and to the promotion of that which affirms the full humanity of women as well as men. The 'prophetic principle', as seen *par excellence* in the Bible in the Hebrew prophets and the life and teaching of Jesus, involves the critique of that oppressive religion which holds in place the ideological legitimation of the status quo, of political, social and economic oppression. There is a clear correlation between these two principles of critique. The prophetic principle, she asserts, is normative and central to biblical religion and 'the feminist interpretation of prophetic critique as feminist critique thus continues the process of scriptural hermeneutic itself, whereby the text is interpreted in the context of new communities of critical consciousness' (122). In this way of looking at the Bible the pastoral theologian is able to engage a serious commitment to the biblical text and its message with a commitment to the priority of issues of wholeness and justice for women.

Deconstruction and Reconstruction
The feminist biblical scholar Elisabeth Schüssler Fiorenza finds 'correlation' too abstract a principle. What is needed, she argues, is the critical evaluation of *particular* texts, and of particular interpretations and traditions of interpretation, of their ideological underpinning and functioning. An excellent example of her method is her examination of Rom. 16, in which historical reconstruction and challenge to androcentric translation combine to give us 'a glimpse of the rich social mix of early Christian communities, as well as of women's contribution to early Christian life and mission' (Schüssler Fiorenza 1990: 71). Schüssler Fiorenza's contribution to feminist biblical interpretation covers an enormous range.[5] She moves through deconstruction of the biblical text—its

---

5.   *In Memory of Her: A Feminist Theological Reconstruction of Christian Origins* (1983); *Bread Not Stone: The Challenge of Biblical Interpretation* (1984); *But She Said: Feminist Practices of Biblical*

androcentic language, its revelations 'between the lines' of the lives and ministries and voices of women, its potential to reveal the hidden history of the
'discipleship of equals' called forth by Jesus (1983: 154)—to reconstruction
involving critical evaluation and proclamation. She argues that:

> Feminist biblical studies…must deconstruct the dominant paradigms of biblical
> interpretation and reconstruct them in terms of a critical rhetoric that under-
> stands biblical texts and traditions as a living and changing heritage, one which
> does not legitimate patriarchal oppression but can foster emancipatory practices
> of faith communities (1992: 5).

Schüssler Fiorenza advocates a hermeneutic that involves *suspicion, proclama-*
tion, remembrance and *creative ritualization.* Particularly helpful for the pastoral
theologian is her dual emphasis on both deconstruction and reconstruction.
The attention to suspicion and deconstruction forcefully presents and illustrates in terms of particular texts the need always to listen to what is not said
and to read between the lines. This need goes far beyond the biblical text into
the writings, the preaching and the public discussions of the Christian community. As a student protested at the end of our sessions on feminist hermeneutics, 'I can no longer hear or read *anything* without wondering what is
not being said!' On the other hand, the attention to liberative interpretation by
communities seeking to live out the discipleship of equals, 'those men and
women in biblical religion who struggle for liberation from patriarchal oppression' (1992: 5), gives space for a positive appropriation of the Scriptures of the
Christian community. The imaginative dimension to the process of creative
ritualization releases the reader (and in particular the pastoral theologian) to
'play' with the text, to bring out hidden dimensions and hidden questions and
also to allow a powerful interplay between the world of the feminist interpreter and the world of the text. That interplay includes the aesthetic and the
emotional.

Kath Saltwell, as student on the Feminist Perspectives course, wrote an
imaginative deconstruction and reconstruction of the incident recorded in
Luke's Gospel (7.36-50) where an unnamed woman washes Jesus' feet with her
tears.[6] Writing on the positive value of women's tears, she seeks to deconstruct
the 'sexist ideology and theological anthropology which have allowed women to
be seen as emotional, irrational beings' and to reconstruct the woman's weeping
in a way that brings out positively the range of fruitfulness of her tears:

Interpretation (1992); *Sharing Her Word: Feminist Biblical Interpretation in Context* (1998).

6.   Quoted here with permission.

> Years of pent-up emotion spilled from me in a torrent, unchecked. As I wept my
> tears of confession, I remembered all the wrong I had done. As I wept tears of
> anger and resentment, I remembered all the wrongs that had been done to me,
> and to women like me. As I wept tears of grief I remembered losses; my lost life,
> my lost identity and lost voice.

This of course raises the question of the Christian canon, and of how the words of Scripture are related to both the creative imaginings of the interpreters of Scripture and indeed also to the writings and scriptures of other religions and philosophies. The concept of an authoritative canon, and of the fact that 'canonical authority has been established in and through the silencing and exclusion of women and other marginalized people' (Schüssler Fiorenza 1993b: 10), is problematic for feminist pastoral theologians, given their commitment to hear silenced and marginalized voices. Some find that the deliberate transgression of canonical boundaries is the key to opening up new possibilities for the Christian Scriptures to live, and for the breath of the Spirit to touch us. Others have a concept and a lived practice of the authority of the Bible in our lives which make this impossible.

The Bible in Global Context
I was recently at a conference organized by the World Council of Churches at which women leaders in theological education from all over the world were present. In the mornings we had a Bible study, led in turn by women from Japan, Switzerland, Canada, Lebanon and Kenya. Hisako Kinukawa from Tokyo began by leading us through some simple origami. The colourful paper, she said, was like a piece of Bible text, which we needed to work on so that something was made of it. She then led us through the story of Ruth in the Bible, displaying in particular the issues related to living in a multifaith context, issues of living together, of empathy, of choosing our paths and of expanding our understanding:

> I wish to learn the depth and flexibility of [Ruth's] faith… The words of Ruth
> ['your God is my God'] are the evidence of God's endless flexibility and broad-
> ness. It shows us, in concrete, what it means to accept the people of other faiths
> and to understand ourselves and each other coming from different parts of the
> world with different social locations (Kinukawa: forthcoming).

The manner in which Hisako Kinukawa conceived what Bible study is, the subjects which interested her, and the interpretative lens through which she read the story, were all related to the context of her living and doing theology in Japan. However, her interpretation of the story of Ruth was not for this reason only of relevance to Japanese or other people from the Asia; the questions arising in one context opened up and enriched the questions those of us from other contexts then brought to the text. For example, as a British woman whose cultural background is virtually exclusively Christian I appreciated the challenge to open myself to the cultural diversity which is so feared in Britain, and also that I was given the model of a faithful way of doing this.

These two aspects—the importance of contextual interpretation of the Bible, and the enrichment of sharing those contextual understandings—have acquired key significance in recent feminist biblical hermeneutics. Schüssler Fiorenza writes of the project of *Searching the Scriptures*:

> [The authors] have also been asked to reflect on how their own particular social locations and political engagements impinge on their feminist perspectives and shape their biblical interpretations. In this way, I hope this commentary project provides a discursive forum in which different and even contradictory voices can define the outline and shape of a *feminist* biblical interpretation (1993b: 18).

As 'different, and even contradictory voices' engage with the biblical text the issue emerges of potential suppression of marginalized voices by dominant feminist voices. Suppression of interpretative voice is clearly linked to a wider social, cultural and economic oppression. This question has been raised sharply in relation to the anti-Judaism latent in interpretations that exalt the liberative praxis of Jesus and the early Christian church over against an uncritical description of the contemporary Judaism as patriarchal and legalistic (Plaskow 1993; Fontaine 1997: 94-95). Dominant European and American feminist voices are likewise challenged by postcolonial readings, as Kwok Pui-Lan illustrates in her reading of the story of the Syro-Phoenician woman. She notes that, 'a feminist reading should not simply emphasize the sex–gender system that is at work in the story, but also pay attention to the intersection of class, race, ethnicity and other factors' (1997: 215).

Feminist biblical hermeneutics started out in *solidarity* with women's experience of oppression. As the diversity of women's situations and contexts has been recognized the discipline has moved through an understanding that there are different ways of 'cutting the cake' of solidarity and into a phase where *fluidity* is a better characterization.

Fluidity and Strategy

Post-structural and postmodern emphases in feminism have thrown into relief the necessity to pay attention to the multiple identities of both biblical characters and their feminist interpreters. Likewise many feminist interpreters invite us to forge shifting alliances between feminist biblical criticism and other feminist practices and theories, between gender, class and ethnicity analyses, and between feminist analysis and a more 'gender-neutral scholarly environment' (McKay 1997: 82; Milne 1997).

Within this movement a specific issue emerges of the relationship between confessional and non-confessional biblical scholarship (Milne 1997). Much early feminist biblical work was done by scholars anchored in a relationship, albeit a highly critical one, to the Christian tradition and the Christian church, and this tradition persists. Some feminist biblical scholars, however, have emphasized rather the ideological (Exum 1994) and political (Bal 1989) entailments of the reading of the text and also its literary features and history of multiple interpretations (Jasper 1998). Within contemporary feminist biblical scholarship a non-confessional approach, with its roots in the secular academy, is strong. 'The non-confessional approach presupposes only that the bible is the product of human literary creativity' (Milne 1997: 57).

This use of the biblical text is characterized by Elisabeth Castelli as 'strategic' rather than 'redemptive':

> Some feminist interpreters take as their main objective the redemption of religious texts, trying to answer the question: How can this text be useful in the contemporary setting? I have taken a different position, still asking how one might make use of the text in a contemporary setting, but having that use be strategic rather then redemptive. How, I have asked, can these texts help us to think about theory, power, solidarity, and resistance around the crucially reorientating categories of gender, ethnicity, race, and class which dominate cultural thinking today? (1994: 296).

In the context of feminist pastoral theology the confessional and with it the redemptive approach to biblical interpretation is by far the most common. It is, however, important to examine and understand the 'strategic' approach. This is first because even for many people of Christian commitment the categories 'confessional' and 'redemptive' have been and are oppressively authoritative. 'Redemption' is not at first sight an oppressive category, but may in fact be such, in so far as it implies within many confessional stances an acceptance of a personal state of unworthiness and sin, defined by others, from which others dictate the way to be free. The reaction of my theological college student who preferred not to have the Bible read (Chapter 2) is an example of this phenomenon. The second reason to take the non-confessional strategic approach seriously is that is allows the full weight of the feminist critique of society and religion to bear on our understanding of the Bible, and does not permit premature closure of questions on the grounds that they are out of court for Christian faith. It may well be that reading in this way with courage and open-mindedness brings its own, somewhat different, 'redemption' of the texts for us.

Is the Bible Abusive?

Recently a friend of mine discussed with me the passage on which he was to preach the following Sunday in church. It was from Hos. 2, in which the prophet describes unfaithful Israel as a prostitute, unworthy of God's love but still tenderly wooed and loved. This passage contains imagery of violence, sexual domination and disgust at women's sexuality—'I will strip her naked and expose her as on the day she was born' (v. 3), 'I will uncover her shame in the sight of her lovers, and no one shall rescue her out of my hand' (v. 10). It also contains imagery of great beauty and tenderness, which, however, takes on a frightening edge to any who are familiar with the double-edged behaviour of the abuser—'I will now allure her, and bring her into the wilderness' (v. 14). These words, and words like them in other parts of the prophetic writings, have been subjected to a feminist critique (Yee 1992) which must be taken seriously, even if a more positive reading of the passages is also made. It must be taken seriously because of the deeply ingrained attitudes to women and their sexuality fostered by such imagery, and also because of the connections of this with abuse. Or so I argued. Neither my friend nor the man who preached in my own church really believed me enough to act on it. The very week following I was in a committee meeting. I had made clear my decision to teach in one particular place rather than another, somewhat to the displeasure of a particular clergyman who described my action publicly, and with no sense of impropriety, as 'whoring off to Oxford' (place name changed). That could only have happened in a context where the language of the Bible was inhabited and internalized. My daughters in their early twenties are immersed in current secular discourse, in which there are plenty of words for sexual behaviour, but the metaphor of 'whoring' for general unfaithfulness was utterly foreign to them. It belongs to the world of the Bible as appropriated in sermons, Bible reading and Christian literature. This was a blatant example of the discourse and imagery of the prophets transferred with utter naturalness into a committee meeting in a theological college context. It brings to life Hampson's contention, previously quoted, that the biblical language may be 'profoundly damaging to human relations'.

This incident raises a host of issues for pastoral theology. There is the issue about preaching. It is vitally important that where the Scriptures are read, and treated with reverence, and used to shape the consciousness of the community, that the dangers of the worldview and language present or potentially present are clearly pointed out. There is also the undeniable evidence that the Bible shapes the thought patterns and language and reality structures of the community that uses it. This example complements those where violent biblical language is used explicitly to legitimize violence against women. In this case no physical violence was in question, and the whole context was overtly ordered and respectable (interestingly no one else even noticed what had been said until I pointed it out, which was a telling corroboration of its 'naturalness'). But that a man can use such language about a woman in this way is intolerable, because it is the 'respectable' end of the whole edifice of patriarchy and patriarchal attitudes which are built on the maintenance of gendered authority, supported by violence, overt and covert and sexualized. 'They have read their Bibles and in doing so inhaled the toxic fumes of the patriarchal ethos of the biblical tradition' (Fontaine 1997: 88).

The notion of an 'abusive' Bible is difficult for many people. That the Bible has been used to abuse, and used by abusers, is well-known. Carole Fontaine's article 'The Abusive Bible' (1997) usefully sets out both evidence for this and also a challenging discussion of the reasons for it. This is something which pastoral carers as well as theologians need to address. Fontaine locates the problem in three areas—the *nature*, the *content*, and the *function* of the Bible (p. 91). Of these by far the most contentious is that the *nature* of the Bible is abusive. That the Bible has *functioned* abusively in the way it has been used (and abused) to maintain the submission and the devaluing of women (as well as of other groups such as colonized peoples, Black people, slaves, gays and lesbians) may be attributed to the distorted ideologies and the 'sin' of Christian communities and others. That some of the *content* of the Bible reflects abusive attitudes and practices is readily recognized by many—for example the treatment of Lot's daughters (Gen. 19. 8), the killing of Jephthah's daughter (Judg. 11), or many of the things said about women in 1 Timothy. In this latter case I remember vividly, well before my days of feminist consciousness, a friend listening in church to the reading of 1 Tim. 4.11-16 and saying that if she were a widow she would walk out of church right now:

> But refuse to put younger widows on the list, for when their sensual desires alienate them from Christ, they want to marry, and so they incur condemnation for having violated their first pledge. Besides that, they learn to be idle, gadding about from house to house; and they are not merely idle, but also gossips and busybodies…(vv. 11-13).

Imagine someone newly widowed coming to church, perhaps for the first time after the funeral—pastoral disaster would be an understatement.

To make the further move, however, to say that the Bible by its *nature* is abusive is a bridge too far for many. This point of view is based partly on a recognition that the Bible contains emancipatory and health-giving elements as well as the more damaging material. For some also it is based on a belief in the authority of the Bible as the revealed Word of God, which belief is supported by personal experience of the life-giving power of the Scriptures. Among feminist biblical scholars and interpreters themselves there is, as has been shown above, a distinction between those who would struggle to identify the redemptive elements in the Scriptures, and those whose hermeneutic is rather strategic and non-confessional. For many pastors and Christians outside the world of feminist scholarship and thinking, even those feminist biblical interpreters who take the 'redemptive' approach seem to have taken a fundamentally inappropriate step by judging Scripture from experience not vice versa. Although, as explained above, I think this is a false dichotomy, the fact remains that this struggle with the meaning of the 'authority of Scripture' is hugely important to people trying to make sense out of the feminist critique from a conservative Christian background. It is the single most important issue which arises in my teaching, and I teach in an ecumenical federation where a wide variety of Christian traditions are represented. The presenting question is: 'Is the Bible itself abusive, or is it a matter of wrong and sinful interpretation?' I should like to make four points by way of contribution to this debate.

First, when the Bible itself is described as abusive what is often meant is that the view some people have of the Bible's authority allows it to have an abusive effect. Fontaine's condemnation of the nature of the Bible is in part actually a condemnation of one particular view of the Bible. She writes that:

> It is precisely because religious communities have held a privileged view of the Bible's 'nature' as some sort of divine product with divine content and purpose that it has been so difficult to analyze the ways in which the Bible might be contributing to the various oppressions visited upon different groups (1997: 92).

It is the use of the Bible as a weapon in the ideological legitimation of oppressive religion which is the problem. Here we are back not to nature but to use, although 'use' in a sense that impinges on what its nature is deemed to be. There is, nevertheless, an even more radical view, also expressed by Fontaine, that the Bible is 'the words of elite males projected on to deity to protect and legitimate the powers of patriarchy' (p. 93). If that is *all* the Bible is, then indeed it is the Bible itself which is by its nature abusive. Here, where this view meets the view of the Bible as bringing the life-giving Word of God, is the point where those of us who both inhabit the Christian tradition and recognize the feminist critique must wrestle with the issues at their sharpest.

Second, the Bible itself is a site of struggle. The oppressor is found within the text, and the liberator is found within the text. This may be illustrated from two quite different examples. Itumeleng Mosala, writing from the context of Black theology in apartheid South Africa, identifies explicitly, encoded within the biblical texts, both perspectives of oppressing class groups and perspectives of the oppressed (Mosala 1989). Mary Hayter, writing in the context of the debate about women and priesthood in the Church of England, identifies in the New Testament a strand of teaching emphasizing women's and men's equality (represented by Gal. 3.28) and a strand of subordinationist theology (represented by the 'household codes' such as Eph. 5.22–6.9). In deciding between these strands she argues that what is new in Christ, what is christological, is what is definitive for Christians and should be accepted as normatively Christian (Hayter 1987). This view implicitly accepts the Bible as a site of struggle. The text contains within itself witness to the diversity of human commitments and religious responses at the time of writing. Its nature therefore is to be ambiguous and open to diverse interpretation.

Third, it is impossible to give a blanket answer to the question concerning whether it is the Bible itself or its interpretation which is the problem, given the clearly patriarchal nature of the contexts in which the Bible was originally written, was then interpreted through history, and is read, heard and interpreted today. These contexts and factors act in a mutually reinforcing way to compound the initial problem. A text that is written in a patriarchal context and then interpreted in a different but still patriarchal context is subject to this reinforcement. Under these circumstances it is very difficult to isolate some pure thing which the Bible 'is'—its 'nature' independent of its use and interpretation.

Finally, therefore, there is a need for nuanced analysis and interpretation which takes individual texts and interpretations in context and allows for a multiplicity of provisional and contested answers. Such specific attention must take into account not only the textual and contextual details, and those things which are hidden between the lines of the text, but also the complexity of how both power and emancipation actually work in particular religious contexts. The woman I mentioned earlier who said in class that her husband justified his beating of her by claiming this was encouraged in the New Testament texts, went on to say, 'But the Holy Spirit told me he was wrong!' Pastoral theology must take account of the full range of religious experience, including the appearance of emancipation in contexts which might otherwise indicate oppression.

The Bible and Liturgy

Worship and liturgy are a particularly important context in which the Bible actually functions for Christian communities. I propose to look briefly at three aspects of the use of the Bible in liturgy and worship to identify some important issues for the feminist pastoral theologian.

There is a complex interaction between the Bible, Christian doctrine and liturgical practice. This can be seen particularly clearly in the connections between the following three factors: *biblical* images and portrayal of sacrifice and of Jesus' death on the cross, the *doctrine* of the Atonement, and the *liturgical celebration* of the Eucharist. In particular, the language of sacrifice used to interpret Jesus' death, to make remembrance of his death in the eucharistic ritual, and to invite the congregation to give their lives in service, is problematic for many women (Procter-Smith 1995a, especially ch. 6). Feminists have long been wary of the language of service and sacrifice, as in practice in society and church it has so often been women who have been used to serve men, and asked to sacrifice themselves for men (Saiving 1995; Ramsay 2000). More than that, abused women find imagery of sacrifice and the exaltation of suffering ambiguous or indeed horrific (Procter-Smith 1995a: 116-17; 1995b). Here the pastoral theologian must be sensitive to issues of biblical interpretation and doctrine as seen through the lens of the pastoral effects of liturgical practice. The Bible does not stand free; it is inextricably implicated in practices.

A further example of this can be seen in the matter of Bible translation. A certain amount can be done to rid translations of unnecessary linguistic sexism, but the patriarchal nature of the social and religious reality which the Bible reflects will show through unless we engage in radical alterations of the text. It is tempting to take the line of the Old Testament scholar John Barton that it is dishonest to clean up the Bible and pretend it is not sexist. What we rather need to do is to 'adopt a lower view of its authority; then we shall be free to let it say what it says, even where we do not like it' (Barton 1992: 550). There is, however, a problem with this approach; the Bible functions as a sacred text, and as such is accorded a privileged position. Barton's position may be a perfectly reasonable one for scholarly study of the Bible, but the way the Bible functions as a community- and life-shaping text is not amenable to such an approach. While I am sure it is essential to preserve versions of the Bible that allow access to the original as far as possible, I am not so sure that it is appropriate for a sexist text to be read in church and in private devotion as life-shaping sacred Scripture.

So the issue of translation does not stand on its own but is linked to the questions surrounding the actual use of the Bible in church services. Here its authority is reinforced by the rituals that surround liturgical reading. The Bible is carried in first while all stand, or it is kissed and held up. Furthermore it is proclaimed as the 'word of the Lord', and preached from a pulpit 'six feet above contradiction', often with a special prayer beforehand (Procter-Smith 1993). That we should have rituals as a mark of respect and pleasure in the good news of God's love is clearly not the problem. The problem is that all these practices and gestures inculcate in people an attitude of dependency and unquestioning acceptance which allows neither for the serious challenging of 'authorities' and of that which damages, nor for exploration of new ways of understanding the nature and message of the Bible.

A feminist pastoral theology will explore how the community (the whole community including women) may be built up by the preaching of the Bible. The reinforcement of authority is not the only possibility opened up by the liturgical context of Bible reading. For example, a former student of the Feminist Perspectives course, a Methodist minister, tells how her studies in feminism and in biblical hermeneutics have led her to hold her own ministry of preaching accountable to her congregation and open to discussion and dispute. She continually puts forward both implicit and explicit invitations to the whole community to join in the enterprise of interpreting the Bible, offering her skills but denying that they (or indeed her status) put her beyond contradiction. Another possibility is to give honest attention in public worship and preaching to the difficult and potentially negative texts in the Bible. A feminist approach to preaching as a way of building up the community would involve asking the hard questions of texts, and addressing them (as in the example of the negative sexual imagery in Hosea referred to above.)

There are both possibilities for positive proclamation and strategic opportunities for dealing with negative texts (Procter-Smith 1993); the question then becomes: 'How much influence and control do women have over the choice of readings, the compilation of lectionaries, the manner in which preaching is conducted, the way in which the Bible is used in churches?' It is to this fundamental level of power that the questions raised concerning the translation of the Bible and its use in public worship lead back.

'Flashes of Alternative Possibilities'

I want to end this chapter on a positive note. I have dwelt at length on the serious questions concerning the use and abuse of Scripture in pastoral contexts, particularly where women are concerned. I have also drawn attention to the questions raised concerning the nature of the Bible. I have tried in this chapter to fulfil the promise of the Introduction to 'visit traditional Christian theological sources and beliefs with an awareness of the acute seriousness of the problems raised in Chapter 2'. But there is a positive side also to be put.

Every year I am astonished that the effect of a rigorous presentation of the feminist critique of the Bible followed by permission to comment on a passage of choice from a feminist perspective calls forth in the majority of students a positive imaginative engagement which proves deeply fruitful in their ongoing lives. In a recent discussion group with women from the course over the last six years the predominant memory of the biblical work was of being set free to enter a new depth and dimension of spirituality, *within the already held tradition*. Clearly this is a phenomenon experienced in a confessional context. This is the context in which feminist pastoral theology operates.

I would therefore agree substantially with the judgment of Elsa Tamez that:

> The tendency of some First World radical feminists to reject the Bible is…an exaggerated reaction. I think that by assigning too much importance to these peripheral texts, many leave aside the central message, which is profoundly liberating. From my point of view, it is precisely the gospel's spirit of justice and freedom that neutralizes antifemale texts (Tamez 1988: 176).

While I would not share Elsa Tamez's view that the difficult texts are 'peripheral', I do share her positive hope in the core gospel message of justice and freedom. She speaks from a context of South American liberation theology. I speak from a quite different Western context and a quite different spirituality, but in this context too the 'spirit of justice and freedom' may be found. A recent sermon in my local church (given by a man) focused on Mary Magdalene, not as the penitent sinner and reformed prostitute of traditional interpretation, submissive, lying fallen on the floor, but as a woman of experience, of independent means, someone who had known personal and communal suffering, a faithful disciple and a witness to the resurrection. This was a good and empowering female role model to hold up to the congregation. Personally I was enlightened, affirmed and challenged by it.

The tools of biblical criticism as forged by mainstream male scholarship will not dismantle the 'abusive Bible'. In a deeper sense, however, we must ask whether the 'master's house' of patriarchal Christian religion may be dismantled by the Bible itself. Not, I think, by itself unaided. But it may be *a* tool among others, and a powerful one at that. At the end of her article on the abusive Bible Fontaine suggests that, 'we deal with the Bible because we *must* and because it is *ours*' (1997: 111). We must deal with the Bible for the reason outlined by Cady Stanton; since the Bible is used to determine the status of women we must therefore challenge unjust practices which are built upon it. In some contexts this applies to society in general, in others only to the world of Christian communities. But the Bible is also *ours*. One of the great contributions of the work of Rosemary Radford Ruether is her insistence that we must both look to the future in hope and to the past in a kind of critical solidarity. Although the Christian tradition, and the Bible within it, is by no means the only source of grace and truth and liberation, we nevertheless need a base from which to start—a base which is our own. Or, in Ruether's own words:

> The effort to express contemporary experience in a cultural and historical vacuum is both self-deluding and unsatisfactory. It is self-deluding because to communicate at all to oneself and others, one makes use of patterns of thought, however transformed by new experience, that have a history… To find glimmers of…truth in submerged and alternative traditions through history is to assure oneself that one is not mad or duped (Ruether 1983: 18).

This critical appropriation of our own tradition is what I believe Christian feminist pastoral theologians need to do with the Bible. 'There are', as Ruether rightly says, 'indeed many flashes of alternative possibilities, that included women, in past periods of Christianity' (Hampson and Ruether 1987: 19). Our wrestling, our struggle, with God includes a struggle with our own Scriptures.[7]

---

7.   Such wrestling and struggle is amply demonstrated in the Scriptures themselves, for example Jacob (Gen. 32) and Job.

Chapter Four

In Whose Image?

Introduction

What does it mean to say that we are made 'in the image of God'? What sort of theological work has this doctrine been made to do and what sort of work should we use it to do? These are current theological questions which go beyond the agenda of feminist pastoral theology. But they are central to a feminist pastoral theology which seeks to explore the intertwined roots of Christian beliefs about God on the one hand and gender-contoured practices on the other.

Traditionally 'the image of God' has been related to creation, to Christology, to eschatology and future hope. Genesis 1.27 has been a key text for Christians:

> So God created humankind in his image,
> in the image of God he created them;
> male and female he created them.

In Christian theology the image of God is also deeply connected with Jesus Christ: 'He is the image of the invisible God' (Col. 1.15). It is therefore a vision of what Christians are to become in Christ: you 'have clothed yourselves with the new self, which is being renewed in knowledge, according to the image of its creator' (Col. 3.10). Recently also the trinitarian nature of God has been used as a model of what it means to be made in the image of God as persons in relation, as the created and renewed community in the image of God (Hilkert 1995: 200).

The following three chapters should be seen as a whole, an exploration from three different angles of the belief that human beings are made in the image of God. In Chapter 4 this is explored from the perspective of the doctrine of God and Christology; in Chapter 5 from the perspective of Christian views of sin and salvation, of what it means to be a whole and good person;

and in Chapter 6 from the perspective of church and community. These topics might be viewed as too much part of the conventional Christian system to be sufficiently radical to hold the insights of feminist theology. I am sensitive to this possibility, but my aim is to encourage a conversation between feminist pastoral theology and care on the one hand and the Christian tradition on the other. I wish to relate to traditional categories in the hope that '[a]s feminist theology systematically corrects the androcentrism of each category of Christianity…the alternative possibilities of the Christian pattern of theology for a liberation theology for women will come into focus' (Ruether 1983: 38). There are some preliminary issues which will be explored in this introduction, which should be seen as an introduction to all three chapters.

Talking about God—the Problem of Ideology
Human constructions of God—the way people talk about God—are bound to reflect human society and human values. These constructions of God in turn—these images, that language—legitimate certain ways of constructing human community; and so it goes on, round in a circle. Images belong with mirrors and reflections, and they involve a two-way process. Or as Bob Dylan expressed it:

> And he worships at the altar of a stagnant pool
> And when he sees his reflection he is fulfilled.

It is here, in this pool, this mirror, this circle, that issues about gender-inclusiveness in the human community connect with issues about how we should speak of and portray God. We have two realities which, when set side by side with one another, create a mutually reinforcing situation. The first reality is that we live in societies where manifestations of male power (social, symbolic, psychological, institutional and economic) constantly overwhelm or threaten to overwhelm the attempts we make to create a just and gender-inclusive community. The second reality is that Christians belong to a religious tradition which treasures as normative Scriptures, stories, symbols and language which have been shaped in societies also dominated by male power, and in which God is portrayed in masculine imagery. What was done in the past is regarded in Christian debate as a warrant for what must be normative for the future. So past and present powers reinforce each other, human practices and religious beliefs legitimate one another. This is how ideology operates. 'If God is male, then the male is God' (Daly 1986: 19). We might also say, 'If the male is God, then God is male'.

It is this situation which leads Daphne Hampson and others to regard Christianity as irretrievably damaging to healthy human relationships and community. Those, like Rosemary Radford Ruether, who would resist this conclusion, point to the ways in which Christianity is not just a religion set in historical concrete, but a faith open to God's future and to the hope of transformation. We cannot transform human community without the transformation of how we think about and portray God. The two indeed go together. The transformation of human relationships is inextricably bound up with the transformation of our vision of God because of the ideological reinforcement and legitimation which happens as our practices and our religious beliefs interact.

A colleague of mine who teaches liturgy is wont to introduce the topic of gender-inclusive language in the following way. Participants are invited to place themselves somewhere on a line which has four key stages in our attitude to the language of the liturgy: stage 1, no change; stage 2, use gender-inclusive language for the human community; stage 3, increase our range of images for God to include, for example, feminine biblical imagery for God; stage 4, change traditional male imagery and symbolism for God, for example the trinitarian formula of 'Father, Son and Holy Spirit'. The inevitability of the ideological process means that to stop at stage 2 is impossible. If the language in which God is conceived and addressed is consistently masculine then the practices of the communities that use it will reflect the higher status, value and 'godlikeness' of men. In such a situation tinkering with gender-inclusive language for the human community is merely treating symptoms, not tackling the causes of the problem.

How God is imaged is related to how human beings are regarded, and the global situation of violence against women and the undervaluing of women make this issue a matter of life and death. It is not a feminist 'fad' about 'political correctness'. It is a matter of understanding the vital nature of the question and the lethal harm done by getting wrong our vision of God and its relationship to human community. The way in which we conceive what it is to be 'divine' involves practical results which are desperately serious and potentially damaging to human beings. The question of value is intimately linked to the question of godlikeness. It is clear that globally, including within Christian communities, women are valued less than men—and there is a direct connection between the value given to human life and that life being seen 'in the image of God'. This lack of value may be experienced as deprivation of food and medical resources, or as violent abuse. It may also be experienced as exclusion from religious roles where the representation of God is at stake, or as alienation and the impossibility of representing one's own experience within the dominant religious discourse and imagery.

Gender and God

It is traditionally asserted that God is 'beyond gender'. This is helpful in so far as it is a witness against the overidentification of male human beings with God, given the prevalence of masculine imagery for God. It is more problematic in the light of contemporary understandings of how gender is an integral part of identity. What does it mean to be made in the image of God if God does not share such an important part of our identity and self? The issue of God and gender identity is, however, not new. The early Christians wrestled with this question, specifically in relation to Gen. 1.27 (Ruether 1974). The Greek tradition, as represented by Gregory of Nyssa (d.c. 395) asserted that the third clause of the verse, 'male and female he created them', was separate from the earlier two clauses, and not to be taken as a further explication of them. Thus sexual identity is not an integral part of the image of God in human beings. Transcending our sexual nature is part of transformation into the image of the creator, and indeed of Christ, whose virginity in this case is considered paradigmatic. Virginity, in men and women, is the condition in which this image is most nearly realized. The Western tradition, on the other hand, as expressed formatively in Augustine (d. 430), asserts that 'male and female' is indeed integral to the image of God. But a differentiation is made between the two. Male and female are complementarily in the image of God; male and female together make up the image of God. The male, however, represents 'reason' in this complementarity, the female 'body'. A dualism of unequal value is set up. What is more, the male may alone represent the image of God; the female may not:

> [T]he woman, together with her own husband, is the image of God, so that the whole substance may be one image, but when she is referred to separately in her quality as a helpmeet, which regards the woman alone, then she is not the image of God, but, as regards the man alone, he is the image of God as fully and completely as when the woman too is joined with him in one (Augustine *De Trinitate* 7.7.10 quoted in Ruether 1974: 156).

This view is mediated down the Western tradition, for example through Aquinas and Barth (Børresen 1991: 222; Ruether 1991: 282).

Neither of these understandings is wholly satisfactory for theology. If 'male and female' is detached from the image of God then our sexuality and gender identity are removed from the divine sphere. Where it is asserted that men and women complementarily make up the image of God, the potential for complementarity to slip into domination would appear to be clearly realized. We are left with the possibility that individually all human beings are made in the image of God, sexuality included, or that as a whole human community we are made in the image of God, sexuality included. While the question of the 'original meaning' of Gen. 1.27 has its own importance (Bird 1991), the question of interpretation and how that interpretation is used to reinforce practices is even more important for pastoral theology.

Some recent feminist work picks up the theme of sexuality and gender in God, or in 'the divine'. I mentioned in Chapter 1 Graham's use of the French philosopher Luce Irigaray to bring into the heart of feminist pastoral theology the question of 'the divine' and how it is named and known. In discussing the 'image of God' and what it means as a woman to name oneself as made in the image of God, Irigaray's insistence that 'women need a God who shares their specificity, and invites them to perfection and wholeness from that very point' (Graham 1999a: 204) raises a question about the adequacy of insisting on a 'God beyond gender' as an antidote to the 'masculine God'. Likewise Bons-Storm's study of women's silences in pastoral care leads her to this conclusion:

> Without a point of orientation for women in the Deity, women will not know who they are, nor can they communicate authentically with other women. This means no less than that we need a new symbolic system that does not acknowledge the one Male Deity…but instead acknowledges a Divinity-in-diversity… This diversity must be expressed in language and images of God/ess (1996: 130).

Such a perspective, as is also found, for example, in D'Costa's *Sexing the Trinity* (2000), contrasts significantly with the more traditional approach of a writer like Gail Ramshaw in *God Beyond Gender* (1995). Feminist theologians would appear to be divided on whether to pursue a strategy of asserting God's transcendence of sex and gender, or a strategy of asserting the female/feminine to be of the divine.[1]

It is important to notice the way language is both problematic and carefully chosen—the divine, Deity (Bons-Storm 1996), God/ess (Ruether 1983), G-d

---

1.   Elizabeth Cady Stanton, writing in 1885, had no doubts on this matter. She opens her commentary with the following remarks on Gen. 1.26-28: 'Here is the sacred historian's first account of the advent of woman; a simultaneous creation of both sexes in the image of God. It is evident from the language that there was consultation in the Godhead, and that the masculine and feminine elements were equally represented… But instead of three male personages, as generally represented, a Heavenly Father, Mother, and Son would seem more rational.

The first step in the elevation of woman to her true position, as an equal factor in human progress, is the cultivation of the religious sentiment in regard to her dignity and equality, the recognition by the rising generation of an ideal Heavenly Mother, to whom their prayers should be addressed, as well as to a Father' (Stanton 1993 [1885]: 14). Her biblical exegesis may be idiosyncratic, but her grasp of the ideological issue is clear and fundamental.

(Schüssler Fiorenza 1992). The impossibility of conveying what is thought to be true by the use of the word 'God' (shaped as it is by a particular patriarchal understanding and tradition) leads feminists to experiment with different words. I have chosen to use the word 'God' or occasionally 'the divine'. I accept that the meanings given to the word 'God' in much theology and popular religion are not ones I wish to appropriate uncritically. The word 'God', however, both conveys my inheritance of Christian faith, a great deal of which I have no desire to repudiate, and also is sufficiently polyvalent (contested, mysterious and still to be explored) to allow me to wrestle with the serious issues raised in this book.

The Doctrine of God

The Problem

Whatever our sophisticated theological assertions, much ordinary talk about God fails to distance itself sufficiently from portraying God as male. God-talk is male-talk. A few years ago I was at my daughter's graduation dinner. Whether by accident or design I had been placed next to a rather deaf elderly clergyman of decidedly conservative views. For a time I kept the conversation banal, but he was neither a fool nor a coward, and it was only a matter of time before my evasions of the topic of feminist theology risked becoming both explicit and rude. So, with fear and trembling I answered a direct question with the mild suggestion that for some feminists the issue of the naming of God as 'Father' could present a problem. It's amazing how quickly a dinner table can become silent! Worse followed as he explained to me how my suggestion that God was not a father in the obvious and biological sense—however else God might be a father—was quite untrue, since God worked the miracle of the incarnation by creating a sperm in Mary and hence was indeed appropriately described as a biological father. Torn between astonishment, fury, amusement and sheer embarrassment, given the social context, I gave what I thought was a really classy answer—'Surely', I said, 'you can't claim that that is orthodox Christian doctrine?'

'Well', he said, 'it was good enough for the boys in prep school.'

Theologians may assert that God has no biological sex and is not affected by social constructions of gender, but this is not true of human constructions of God. It is not true of human psychological and social projections onto God. And it is not true of the ways in which people talk about God.

I give two further brief examples. I went to the ordination of a friend to the Anglican priesthood and the Bishop preaching described God as 'like a very big bloke'—again, not exactly Cappadocian orthodoxy but a common enough view I think (though that it was held by a Bishop surprised me; I suppose it should not have done). It should not therefore have been a surprise when, at a school religious education class I was invited to address on issues about gender and God, a seventeen-year-old girl was heard to remark to her neighbour, 'But if God isn't a man then everything I have always believed is wrong'.

In these examples the tendency (found among bishops, clergy and lay people) to identify God with the male human person is seen clearly. The very outrageousness of the examples (which were not seen as at all outrageous by those who said these things) is an indication of the prevalence and tenacity of the problem. Such talk betrays beneath its surface a depth of explicit teaching and implicit assumptions which find their way into common parlance as well as into theological discussion and practical church politics. For example, in discussing the question of women's ordination in the Roman Catholic Church Lavinia Byrne writes of the way theological understanding 'has its basis in the symbolic ordering of reality; it says that the Father sends the Son into the world and so it establishes a male chain of command' (Byrne 1994: 103).[2] The roots of this are manifold. They are in part biblical, in part based on the maleness of Jesus Christ, in part based on a certain view of 'God-given' human relations. Hampson quotes C.S. Lewis:

> Suppose the reformer stops saying that a good woman may be like God and begins saying that God is like a good woman. Suppose he says that we might just as well pray to 'Our Mother which art in Heaven'… But Christians think that God Himself has taught us how to speak of Him. To say that it does not matter is to say either that all the masculine imagery is not inspired, is merely human in origin, or else that, though inspired, it is quite arbitrary and unessential (1990: 82).

This way of setting out the matter points to a key issue—the fatherhood of God. Feminists, and particularly those involved in pastoral care, have of course frequently drawn attention to the difficulties of calling God 'father' and attributing to God the qualities of a father. To move from this to calling God 'mother' may well raise as many problems as it solves, since the real issue at stake here is the nature of theological language. The problem is that 'father' is not regarded as metaphorical in the same way that other images for God might be. It is of the nature of a metaphor that we can say both 'is' and 'is not' (Soskice 1987). For example, 'John is a pig' (in so far as John is greedy and ill-mannered) but John is not a pig (in so far as John is not pink with four legs

---

2. The Vatican's Congregation for the Doctrine of the Faith condemned the author of this book and had the book removed from the lists of The Liturgical Press at St John's Abbey, Collegeville, Minnesota.

and a tail). So God both is a rock and is not a rock. God is a mother and is not a mother. God is a father; are people also able to say God is not a father? Normally if I ask this question of a group some say 'yes', some 'no' and some 'don't know'. 'Father' carries a certain authentication when used of God. If pushed people normally related this to the 'Our Father' of the Lord's Prayer, or to the biblical reference to God as 'the father of our Lord Jesus Christ'. If 'father' is a privileged word for God then there will inevitably be slippage in consciousness to the attribution of male characteristics to God and thence to the closer identification of males with God.

All this has important consequences for women's and girls' self-image and spirituality. C.S.Lewis continues the argument quoted above, 'A child who had been taught to pray to a Mother in Heaven would have a religious life radically different from that of a Christian child' (Lewis 1970: 90-91). Indeed she would have a radically different religious life from that of a child taught that God is essentially to be depicted in masculine imagery. Jo Ind writes of her experiences as a Christian teenager suffering from an eating disorder. She tells of the image of 'father' she lives with—a distant unemotional father, whose role took him into a hierarchical, competitive world—and of how this affected her view of God in the light of her eating disorder:

> In the presence of my heavenly father I felt more ashamed of my weakness, not less... When I saw God as masculine I saw the world as a hierarchical structure with the good people at the top and me, a compulsive eater, stuffing miserably at the bottom... When I was a child I saw a sticker on the back of a car saying 'Talk to God. She listens'... I pointed it out to my mother and we agreed that it was blasphemous... But when [as an adult] I considered what 'father' meant to me, a solution appeared in my mind. What if God were my heavenly mother? For surely God was both male and female and neither, because God is a mystery... When I imagined that God was my heavenly mother, the context in which I had an eating disorder changed. It is not an exaggeration to say the whole world became a different place.
>
> I realised that God was close, not distant. She was as close to me as I had been to my earthly mother in the womb... When I came to my heavenly mother and told her about my eating disorder I did not have to explain. I could rest in the presence of the one in whose image I was made. Worries about stretchmarks and thighs had a place—I pictured her as being on the round side herself...nothing I had experienced was alien to her. I rested in the love of one who knew (Ind 1993: 41).

I have quoted this passage at length as it makes so clearly and movingly the point that image of God, self-image, religious life and material life are deeply intertwined, and the appropriation of female imagery for God is essential to the very life and survival of some women. Those who would seek to show that it is not Christian, must then show why Hampson is wrong to say that Christianity is damaging to women.

Resources

This is, however, too pessimistic a conclusion. There are a variety of resources within the Christian tradition upon which to draw in the struggle to express what we understand of God in ways that include women.

Female imagery. While the prevailing biblical and traditional imagery for God is male/masculine, there is a warm stream of female/feminine imagery to be tapped. In the Bible itself God is compared to a mother (Isa. 49.15; 66.12-13), to a woman in labour (Isa. 42.14), to a woman sweeping the floor and looking for lost coins (Lk. 15.8-10). The figure of Wisdom is feminine (Prov. 3.13-18), Wisdom who is identified with the creative Spirit of God (Prov. 8), with the presence of God in this world. Christ also pictures himself as a mother hen, longing to gather her chicks under her wing (Mt. 23.37).[3] More important perhaps than particular texts, is the presentation of qualities in God which may be associated with what are considered women's qualities: nurture, compassion, weeping, tenderness, strength in childbirth. It is difficult to steer a path here between a desire to break down stereotypes and a desire to see how God is identifiable in those 'types' which are regarded as particularly womanish/womanly.

Identification of God, and in particular of Christ, as 'mother' is often associated with the writings of the anchoress Julian of Norwich in the fourteenth century. Caroline Walker Bynum has shown how this image was also prevalent in twelfth-century Cistercian writing, but in so doing has raised the question of what such use of maternal imagery actually tells us:

> The maternal imagery of medieval monastic treatises tells us that cloistered males in the twelfth century idealized the mothering role, that they held consistent stereotypes of femaleness as compassionate and soft (either weak or tender)... But it would be unwarranted to argue that this imagery tells us what monks thought of actual women or of their own mothers (Walker Bynum 1982: 167).

This analysis should alert us to the danger of assuming that female imagery for God in and of itself indicates something healthy or freeing for women. God may be projected in the image of a constructed identity.

---

3.   As famously depicted in the window of the church of 'Dominus Flevit' on the Mount of Olives and reproduced on the cover of this book. See Mollenkott (1986) for a wide exploration of feminine imagery in the Bible.

In more recent times the Shaker movement supplies an interesting example of an attempt to find gender-inclusive imagery for God reflecting an equality of power in earthly gender roles. Linda Mercadante, in her fascinating study of Shaker doctrines of God, examines the three options open to those who would take a gender-inclusive approach to God-imagery. Feminine or female traits may be added on to 'a God still essentially imaged as male or masculine'; God may be seen as 'composed of masculine and feminine elements'; or attempts may be made to image God beyond gendered construction, for example as 'Supreme Intelligence' (Mercadante1990: 164-68). Mercadante's analysis highlights two problems: the need to avoid a 'binitarian' view of God in which stereotypical and culturally constructed notions of 'the masculine' and 'the feminine' are projected onto God, and the need to preserve 'our appreciation of God's essential incomprehensibility' (p. 172).

God's Trinity. I was brought up to call the Holy Spirit 'he'. This was to make clear that the Holy Spirit is a person not an 'it'. But why not 'she'? My teachers would have pointed me to the masculine grammatical gender of the pronoun in John's Gospel; my later feminist mentors to the feminine grammatical gender of the Hebrew and Syriac words for Spirit. Some feminist theologians have found the idea of the Spirit as feminine a helpful antidote to the masculine connotations of Father and Son. I have vivid memories of a (male) student loudly reciting in chapel 'We believe in the Holy Spirit…with the Father and Son she is worshipped and glorified'. While the effect of hearing 'she is worshipped and glorified' is imaginatively liberating I am not sure in the long run much is gained by this use of 'she' for the Holy Spirit. As with attempts to include Mary as a balance to male God-language, the feminine is accorded an ambiguous place, one which is often downplayed by comparison with the 'male' characters. It is better to avoid inadequate 'sexualization' of our image of God, and with it the tendency to incorporate uncritically elements of humanly constructed masculine/feminine roles. I have no great predeliction for the use of the word 'it' but I do think that to preserve precisely the mysterious nature of the Spirit, not identified nor bound by human gender construction, is a witness against improper identification of God with human distortions. Non-gendered language helps us see the limits of our metaphors. If we are to move in the direction of 'sexing the Trinity' (see above) it must be in a more sophisticated and ideologically aware manner than the compensatory inclusion of a 'feminine' Spirit or of the Virgin Mary.

In recent theology the doctrine of God's Trinity is often invoked as showing the truly relational and loving nature of God, which should be the vision upon which human community, including the community of the church, models itself. This vision of God may be helpful to feminist pastoral theologians (Williams 1992: 41). For example, Mary Tanner writes of the World Council of Churches' study process 'Community of Women and Men in the Church', 'We held before us, at almost every meeting, the Rublev icon of the Trinity. The social Trinity was seen to correspond most directly to the most fundamental questionings of women about God' (Tanner 2001: 66).

It is not, however, the case that all theologians who put an emphasis on the trinitarian life of God as the life into which the Christian community is called necessarily see the model as one of equality without hierarchy. Eastern Orthodox theology emphasizes loving relationships as constitutive of the being of God in which the Christian community also has its being. This perspective allows talk of hierarchy where hierarchy refers not to domination but to different roles which reflect how relationships are defined. So, for example, John Zizioulas writes that the church 'becomes hierarchical in the sense in which the Holy Trinity is itself hierarchical: by reason of the specificity of relationship… Hierarchy and authority are thus born out of relationship and not of power…' (1985: 223-24). A 'communion of persons' is held out seriously as a viable alternative to a 'relationship of exploitation'. While this vision is in some authors treated with proper attention to the distorted and ideologically conditioned situation in which human beings live in the world, without a vigorous self-critique it will remain vulnerable to distortions created by the theology, language and practices of the Orthodox Church itself.[4] Nevertheless, this trinitarian theological understanding of human relationships has a significant contribution to make to a critical feminist pastoral theology.

God's Incomprehensibility. The feminist pastoral theologian may draw on positive female imagery in the Christian tradition, and also on models and images which call in question gendered imagery. Furthermore the apophatic tradition in Christian theology (in which God is understood as fundamentally mysterious, unknowable and unnameable) is of great importance. God may only be spoken of through metaphor and analogy and in halting speech. Two consequences of this are of particular interest to feminist pastoral theology: the approach to God through a wide range of images, and the understanding of all images as unstable and historically contingent.

Valerie De Marinis tells of a girl who, forbidden to draw God with two faces, one male and one female, eventually comes to draw God as a dancing

---

4.   See FitzGerald (1999) for a range of Orthodox views.

butterfly (De Marinis 1993: 68-80). The inadequacy of either male or female imagery for God on its own leads to both the incorporation of male and female imagery into a view of God, and also to an imaginative expansion of the ways in which God is thought of, expressed and addressed. An excellent example of this is Janet Morley's book of prayers, *All Desires Known* (Morley 1992), which explores a whole range of ways of conceiving God—'God, intimate and fearful', 'Tender God', 'God our beloved', 'O thou sudden God', 'O God my dark, my silence'.

One reason why metaphors and symbols should not be fossilized is that they change in meaning and significance according to time, place, circumstance and deliberate development. I find Janet Martin Soskice's work particularly helpful here. She analyses the fluidity and changeability of the metaphor of 'father' for God throughout the Hebrew and Christian Scriptures in this way:

> It is not a model there from eternity (the patriarchal father), but a mobile symbol whose sense develops through the Hebrew Bible, and which for Christians takes on a different sense in the books of the New Testament where 'father' is known from the sisters and brothers in Christ to whom God stands as Abba father (Soskice 1992b: 26-27).

In contemporary contexts 'father' may signify a wide variety of meanings, ranging from the violent and abusive to the loving and nurturing. As new metaphors grow (the world as God's body) and old metaphors die (Christians as slaves of God) Christians are faced with the question of how to deal with root metaphors and symbols, including those which have been part of patriarchal abuse. Soskice argues that the community may 'turn the symbols' on the basis of the fluid nature of symbols and of the actual history of symbols in Christianity—for example, the transformation of images of God as judge, king and lord in the Reformed tradition from their use to legitimate domination and violence under apartheid to their use in liberation theology as symbols of freedom under God from all human domination. 'It would seem', she writes,

> that the most successful revolutions of thought and practice occur, not when a whole life-world is overthrown and attempts are made to construct a new symbolic order from scratch, but when the living symbols of faith are turned to become the tools of a new vision and a new life (1996: 30).

Our attempts to speak of God are inevitably caught up in the life, the actions and the reflection of the communities that name God, and it is important to recognize the provisional and partial nature of our comprehension.

Christology

The Problem

Jesus Christ was without doubt a male human being. This presents a series of related problems to feminist theologians, which have been tackled in a rich variety of ways. What is the significance of the male human being, Jesus, for faith? Can a male saviour save women?

I begin with something which happened in 1999 in the institution in which I work. A selection from the slide series The Christ We Share (CMS, USPG, Methodist Church 1999) was shown during our fortnightly worship. The slides were shown on the basis of a shared theological understanding that Jesus Christ reveals the presence of God in all human flesh, indeed some would say in all created matter. He bore the sins of women and of men in his flesh; he brought both men and women to glory. Because of this identification of Jesus Christ with all human beings, artists have felt free to represent Jesus, particularly Jesus dying on the cross, in various ways which are not historically accurate, but are theologically accurate. We saw a black Jesus and a white Jesus on the cross, a calm Jesus and a tortured Jesus, Jesus from different times and from different places—but we did not see a woman Jesus. There was no Christa, in spite of the fact that Edwina Sandys's *Christa* is one of the slides in the set. Although the Christa has become for many a significant sign of the Jesus who suffered on behalf of all, including women, that slide was omitted, presumably lest it offend. Why is it so often considered permissible to suspend historical particularity in respect of everything about Jesus except his sex?

Given not only the fact of Jesus' maleness, but also the way many Christians tenaciously cling to the importance and significance of his maleness, it is not surprising that Christology has been a difficult area for feminist theologians. For the pastoral theologian these issues are of extreme importance, related as they are both to the question of who is allowed to minister in Jesus' name and represent him as his priest, and also to the question of whether women can find a way of salvation in the identification of Jesus with all humanity, when he is seen as clearly more identified with one sort of humanity than with another. Compare the following assessments of Jesus Christ:

> Christology gives a male human being a status which is given to no woman… Indeed it may be (as in my case) because one deeply cares that there should be good and equal relations between men and women that one is adamant that no one human being can be given the kind of status which Christians give to Christ (Hampson 1990: 76).

> Jesus Christ thus represents a three-fold significance: first he identifies with the
> 'little people', Black women, where they are; secondly, he affirms the basic
> humanity of these, 'the least'; and thirdly, he inspires active hope in the struggle
> for resurrected, liberated existence (Grant 1989: 217).

Here are two radically different evaluations of the possibilities for Christology
to make a positive and life-giving contribution to Christian living.

Hampson sees the status given to Christ as inevitably distorting human relationships. This critique is developed in a particular direction by feminist theologians who see Jesus' death on the cross as the story of a lone hero, modelled on
male experience (Hunt 1992: 150) or even worse as the legitimation of suffering. Carlson Brown and Parker indeed describe the possibility of seeing popular
forms of atonement theology as 'divine child abuse' (1989).

By contrast Grant makes a wholly positive assessment of the significance of
Jesus, including, it is implied, his suffering. Jesus is able to identify with those
who are in some respects unlike him—here Black women. Jesus identifies
with those who struggle, and affirms the humanity of those who are counted
least in society. Jesus brings hope of resurrection and liberation. Note here the
strong connection between Jesus and people of today. In one sense his historical particularity doesn't matter (he can identify beyond boundaries of the first-
century Jewish male); in another sense the historical life, deeds, death, and
resurrection of Jesus Christ are central to our knowing him to be this kind of
saviour. Grant speaks from the experience of the history of the suffering of
African American women. Jesus Christ, as historical figure and as symbol, is
incorporated into the struggle of Black women; this is the interpretative lens
through which his meaning for faith and salvation is understood.

The 'turning of symbols' can be seen clearly here. The actual way in which
Jesus has been interpreted and used, in the communities of the women who are
writing, affects their assessment—inevitably and rightly. Hampson refers to the
protracted debates in the Church of England concerning whether women could
represent Jesus Christ in priesthood and leadership when she says 'While men
(and some women) consider whether women can be full insiders within the
church, women debate whether or not they want to be' (Hampson 1990: 4).
This gives a quite different interpretative lens for understanding Jesus' meaning
for faith and salvation from the one used by Grant.

In summary, the following key questions arise for feminist pastoral theologians if we take seriously the connections between human communities and
our view of God. First, Jesus Christ is a central symbol and figure in the Christian faith—and he is male. Because of this the hymns, stories, pictorial art and
symbolism (crucifixes, icons) of the Christian tradition are tied inevitably to the

predominant presence of the male. Furthermore, there is often an 'ontological slippage' in which the human maleness of Jesus is transferred to God his 'father'.

Second, God in Jesus lived the life of a man not a woman. Human life is conceived of as taken up into God through the life of Christ. What points of identification are there between female life and the life of God in Jesus Christ? While classical Christology sought to make clear that God took on human life as a generic category, that category is less easy to sustain today, either philosophically (Hampson 1990) or in terms of our understanding of the radical differences in what it means to be a human being across gendered, cultural and historical divisions. There are clearly a whole range of experiences, and not only those which are gender-related, of which Jesus Christ has no direct personal experience—for example old age, marriage, modern Western city life, slavery or rape. Despite this it is a significant difficulty for feminist pastoral theology that the key Christian narrative has the story of a man's life at its centre.

Third, there is the question of representation. Jesus Christ supposedly represents all humanity; how can he represent women if he himself is constantly represented as male and women are not allowed to represent him? The argument that all humanity is represented by and in Jesus Christ is constantly undermined by accounts of what it is to be a man which identify men more closely with Christ (Martin 1994: 390), specifically by the restriction of Christian priesthood and leadership to men, and by the outcry against imaginative depiction of a woman suffering on the cross.

Resources
Feminist theologians have sought in a variety of ways to offer creative and imaginative solutions to these problems of symbolism, of identification and of representation. A succinct recent summary is provided by Jenny Daggers in her article 'Feminist Theology as Christo/alogical Revisioning' (Daggers 2001). I do not propose here to offer a comprehensive survey, but rather as with feminist strategies of biblical interpretation, to suggest some areas of importance in these debates for feminist pastoral theology. I centre my reflections round three words—hope, imagination and courage. If the story and the understood meaning of Jesus Christ's life, death and resurrection cannot furnish these, then they are of little use to a pastoral theology arising out of reflection on the reality and nature of violence.

Prima facie there should be some clear connections, given the nature particularly of Jesus' death. Recent feminist theology has concentrated particularly on the dangerous possibilities of the glorification of suffering inherent in the story of Jesus' crucifixion, and of the concommittant picture of God meting out violent punishment. However, whatever difficulties arise in the understanding of Christ's death which appear to legitimate violence and abuse (Brock 1988: 56; Carlson Brown and Parker 1989), one factor which does not legitimate violence is clear and significant. Christian tradition identifies God as present and at work in the world in a man who was nailed to a cross not in a man who tortured others. This is fundamentally significant. It is a symbol which we need to 'turn' to good purposes, in a refusal to identify God with the perpetration of violence or cruelty.

Hope of Liberation. 'While some Western feminists have questioned whether a male saviour can save women… Asian feminist theologians are not thus occupied' (Kwok 2000: 85). Although Western feminists are more preoccupied than their African and Asian sisters about the significance of Jesus being male, feminists from a wide variety of perspectives agree in locating Christology within the tradition of liberation theology.[5] The Christian hope can be rooted in Jesus and inspired by Jesus by focusing on his life and his preaching. Jesus was the 'iconoclastic prophet' (Ruether 1981: 54) who proclaimed the love of God for the least and renounced systems of domination, seeking 'to embody in his person the new humanity of service and mutual empowerment' (p. 56). Both Jesus' words and his actions proclaim this message and this hope; women are included in this vision as they are among the least in this world. One might also stress quite specifically the attitude of Jesus to the women around him, and their part in his work. On this reading it does not matter that Jesus was a man. What matters is that Jesus, whose story Christians tell as the story of 'God with us', taught, lived out and was even ready to die for, the truth that God's love is given equally to all and works for the liberation of all. Christians are called to share this work and proclamation. Christian hope is expressed in this story of God's concern for the liberation (redemption/salvation/wholeness) of all people.

The value of this christological perspective is the way it allows women to insert themselves into the classical biblical Christian narrative both as recipients of liberation and as agents of liberation. It also makes the question of Jesus' maleness less relevant. But is there a price to pay for this? There are questions which must be asked. As a fully liberated human being, working and

---

5.   See, for example, the work of Jaqueline Grant, Letty Russell and Rosemary Radford Ruether in North America; Julie Hopkins in Britain; Elsa Tamez in South America; Mary John Mananzan in Asia; and Mercy Amba Oduyoye in Africa (Grant 1989; Russell 1993; Ruether 1981; Hopkins 1995; Tamez 2001; Mananzan 1995; Oduyoye 2001a).

dying for the liberation of others, Jesus is an inspiring example. But can we go further than that and say that what he was and did revealed to us something of the nature of the divine, of God? Can we say we have hope because through Jesus we know what God is like? Can we know that this understanding of what God is like is a true one, representing the ultimate truth of how things are? If we cannot say these things we may live in a hope which is founded only on either wishful thinking or ethical commitment. Maybe these are not bad foundations for hope. But can we have more? By identifying Jesus with God we make the move which allows us to say that God is on the side of the poor, God is the liberator, but in so doing we run straight back into the problem which this Christology was meant to avoid, the identification of a male human being in a unique way with God. To experience the ethical commitment envisaged in this liberationist reading of Jesus fully as hope, some account of resurrection, of the empowerment of God's Spirit, and of the promise of the coming of God's full presence must be embraced.

Imagination. Hope is motivated and understood by means of images and symbols. Christian belief about Jesus Christ, and the hope centred on him, has been expressed in the titles given to him and images used of him such as Messiah, Saviour, Son of Man, Son of God, Logos (grammatically masculine), second person of the Trinity, Lamb of God. Feminist theologians have sought to expand understanding and hope by exploring a range of concepts and images—some gathered from the Christian tradition, some from other religious traditions, and some from women's specific experiences.

Sophia is the Greek word for 'wisdom', grammatically feminine and often portrayed as a woman. It was one of the terms, along with *logos* indicating 'word' and 'rationality', available from existing Jewish and contemporary philosophical and religious sources to the early Christians seeking to give an account of Jesus as the presence of God among human beings in the world. Recently feminists have reappropriated Sophia as a way of understanding Jesus and his work. It is, for example, central to the work of Elizabeth Johnson on the doctrine of God. In *She Who Is* she writes:

> Jesus is Sophia incarnate, the Wisdom of God… Not only does the gender symbolism cast Jesus into an inclusive framework with regard to his relationships with human beings and with God, removing the male emphasis that so quickly turns to androcentrism. But, the symbol giving rise to thought, it also evokes Sophia's characteristic gracious goodness, life-giving creativity, and passion for justice as key hermeneutical elements in speaking about the mission of Jesus (Johnson 1997: 16-17).

The roots of the wisdom tradition are inclusive—encouraging a vision of cosmic significance for Jesus Christ, a broad outlook on human history and dialogue with other religious traditions. 'Wisdom' offers an organic, immanent and creative model of christology (Kwok 2000: 92), bringing imaginative possibilities to a feminist pastoral theology which wants to take seriously ecological concerns as well as concerns for human justice. Mary Grey builds on the Sophia traditions in her emphasis on mutuality, right and just relations, and a theology of flourishing (Grey 1989; 2000a: 49-57; 2001: 100-110). 'Flourishing' will be an important image for understanding the community in the image of God in Chapter 6 of this book.

Images to illuminate our understanding of Jesus Christ are drawn also from quite different religious contexts. Kwok Pui-lan cites the work of Stella Baltazar, an Indian Roman Catholic religious sister, who employs the concept of Shakti, the feminine and creative principle of the universe, to enlarge understanding of Jesus Christ in an Indian context. This way of understanding opens up a feminine dimension of the divine, encourages 'fruitful cross-fertilization' between Indian ecofeminists and Indian Christian theologians, and draws on local cultural roots and religious concepts. Such an example is only one among many which are springing up globally as feminist and other theologians challenge 'the language, models and frameworks used by Western theologians, especially by the male elites' (Kwok 2000: 95).

Finally I mention again an image which is presented not primarily in words but in sculpture or pictures—the 'Christa'—a female Christ on the cross. Such a visual depiction is shocking to many, as it seems to push to the limit our imaginative acceptance that Jesus fully represented women both in his humanity and in his work of overcoming evil. It asks us to take with the utmost seriousness the sense in which Jesus Christ significantly transcends particular identification as a male human being. It invites imaginative engagement with God's identification in Christ with women's sufferings in particular.

Courage.

> The condition of Black people today reflects the cross of Jesus (Grant 1989: 216).

I mentioned right at the start of this section on Christology the words of Jaquelyn Grant which proclaim the significance of Jesus for Black women in America, by contrast, she points out, with some white feminist interpretations of Christ.[6] She speaks of Jesus' identification with Black women, and of his

---

6.   Her book is significantly called *White Woman's Christ and Black Woman's Jesus*. She demonstrates clearly the ways in which the significance of Jesus Christ varies according to

inspiring active hope in the struggle. But this only makes sense in the context of the crucifixion of Black people. For this womanist Christology, Jesus is a political Messiah, a cosufferer: 'His suffering culminated in the crucifixion. Their crucifixion included rape, and babies being sold' (Grant 1989: 212). Such a Christology is not only an account of Jesus Christ; it is precisely as such also an account of the condition of those who are God's people.

There is a strong theme in feminist Christology which sees the liberative and redemptive work of Christ in the work of the 'christic' community (Brock 1988; Ruether 1998). This approach seeks to overcome the individualism inherent in some Christologies, and also to include women in the work of redemption. Although this view does not imply in such a direct way as Grant's womanist account that the community is in a condition of crucifixion, it does imply the need for courage to resist evil. As Ruether says:

> While Jesus is the foundational representative of this way of the cross…he is not its exclusive possibility. Each Christian must also take up this same way and, in so doing, become 'other Christs' to one another. The church becomes this redemptive community…by collectively embodying this path of liberation in a way that transforms people and social systems (Ruether 1998: 93).

Such a path may indeed involve courage and suffering as it did for Christ. I discovered recently at an international women's conference that whereas embodying just practices in theological education for me meant argument; for one of my sisters it meant a personal and deeply hurtful attack on her family. Speaking out against injustice in public life for me meant writing a letter; for one of my sisters meant risking being walled up alive. If the transformation of people and social systems is part of Christology then courage as well as imagination and hope is called for.

Hope Revisited—Resurrection. In the final chapter of her *Introducing Redemption in Christian Feminism* Rosemary Radford Ruether sets out three traditions of the hope for redemption which have influenced Christian belief (1998: 108-109). The first is a historical this-worldly future hope for redemption from servitude into freedom, as exemplified in the Exodus tradition. The second is a hope for an escape from the mortality of the body into the immortality of the soul, as exemplified in the Greek philosophical tradition. The third is a hope for the final triumph of good over evil, involving the resurrection of the dead and cosmic transformation, as exemplified in Persian, Jewish and Christian

---

the history, stories and material conditions of the community which names and appropriates him.

apocalyptic writings. Ruether, as many other feminist theologians, emphasizes hope for this world over individualistic hope for a life beyond the grave. To espouse such hope involves a commitment to justice making and to the flourishing of the earth and the human community. To focus on this world and its flourishing is also to 'accept our mortality and transience, relinquishing the illusion of permanent immortal selves that are exempt from this process [of decay and recycling]' (Ruether 1998: 119).

This contrast sets hope and struggle for justice and flourishing in this world over against an other-wordly hope based on projections of individualistic desire for immortality. But it simply does not address that third tradition, of the resurrection of the dead and the triumph of good over evil. Ruether's perspective enjoins a mixture of acceptance of transience and fight for justice, which allows us to give an account of hope for the present and indeed for the future (in so far as we struggle for a more just future for all), but it gives no account of the past, of the reversal of the injustices and pains in which people lived and died.

Janet Martin Soskice puts this question to Elisabeth Moltmann-Wendel, in response to a paper emphasizing the actions of the historical Jesus:

> Will the rediscovery, the repristinisation, of the human Jesus be enough for beleaguered feminists and, more importantly, for the sufferings of those girls and women who may never in their life read a word of theology? What does it mean for those, more than a hundred million of whose numbers are missing?... Unless I can believe in a risen Christ who somehow—and I don't know how—will redeem these sufferings, as well as promise a better future, I can have no hope (Soskice 1993: 121).

A Christology which has nothing to say to those who suffer and die without ever seeing a world of justice and flourishing cannot address the past and the dead, cannot address the righting of wrongs, cannot champion the triumph of the victim over her executioner, and cannot wipe away tears or bring joy in the mo(u)rning.

What account of resurrection can feminist theology give? Resurrection is not currently a popular feminist theme, as it tends to cut across the desire to emphasize this-worldly hope. In the context of a liberation perspective resurrection is often interpreted as the hope for renewal of justice and community. However, the liberationist feminist preference for concentration on the historical Jesus, rather than the risen and ascended Christ, tends to undercut any sense that such resurrection is part of God's promise or any sense of an underlying reality that, in Bultmann's words, 'the last power is good'. Julie Hopkins unusually devotes a whole chapter to 'The Resurrection and Herstory'

(Hopkins 1995: 64-80). She is clear in her claim that 'In the presence of God we can rise again; the powers of darkness can never overcome the sisters and brothers of radical hope' (p. 72). But she admits that, 'the uniqueness of Christ is not central to such an interpretation, rather the emphasis lies upon the power and presence of God to defeat evil and death and our ability to recognise this' (p. 72). Hopkins thus points to experience (of which the experiences of the original witnesses to Jesus' resurrection are but one example) as the ground for belief in this ultimate triumph of good. Such experience, she claims, gives us true access to how things are. This Christology therefore goes part way to addressing the importance of resurrection for Christian hope, but does not directly tackle the issue of the healing of those who knew no healing or justice in life. Herein lies a question concerning the meaning of history and of human life which feminists must not bypass; there is an agenda here for future feminist Christology.

Chapter Five

A Woman in the Image of God

> To acknowledge gender and sex in the pursuit of pastoral knowledge and practice means analysing the different meanings given to having a male or female body, and trying to find out what it means for a person to live faithfully as a sexual and embodied human being (Bons-Storm 1996: 36).

Sex and bodies have always featured strongly in Christian accounts of what it means to be a woman. Both the myth of feminine evil and the myth of feminine purity are predicated on the fact that women are *female* human beings with female bodies, female sexuality and specifically female characteristics. Christian theological anthropology (the account given of what it means to be a human being) has in the main been structured by attention to two factors. The first is how to give an account of evil, failure, alienation, estrangement and all those features of human existence that cause pain and guilt, including the violence that is the underlying theme of this book. Traditionally Christian theology has structured such reflection around the story of the Fall. The second factor is how to give an account of love, wholeness, goodness and good relationships with God and within the human community—in what do these consist and how are they to be found and lived? Traditionally Christian theology has structured this reflection around the themes of redemption and grace in Christ, in the stories of Incarnation and Atonement. So 'sin' on the one hand and 'salvation' on the other have been key concepts in exploring what it means to be a human being.

My agenda in this chapter is set by Riet Bons-Storm in the quotation above: what does it mean for a woman 'to live faithfully as a sexual and embodied human being'? I shall approach this through an examination of what is seen as women's sin and what is seen as women's salvation. Then I shall address the resulting question of whether women are somehow so different from men that we need a dual rather than a single theological anthropology. Finally I shall revisit the question of humanity in the image of God, and ask what it means for a woman to name herself as made in the image of God.

Sin and Salvation

Sin and salvation are two sides of a coin. Salvation is salvation *from* something, and how that salvation might work out in practice is determined by what it is salvation from. There is a question for women in the Christian tradition—who defines what constitutes sin and what constitutes corresponding salvation? I want to show, first how this dialectic between sin and salvation works, and second how a move has been made from allowing men to define what is women's sin and salvation, to enabling women to define this for themselves and from their own experience.

A Traditional View

One meaning given in the Christian tradition to having a female body is enshrined in the foundational story of a woman, Eve, succumbing to the devil and pulling the man into the same sin, thereby tainting all women through her actions and illustrating the feeblemindedness of women and their potential to tempt men sexually. Tertullian (160–230 CE) said of women:

> You are the devil's gateway: you are she who first violated the forbidden tree and broke the law of God. It was you who coaxed your way around him whom the devil had not the force to attack. With what ease you shattered that image of God: man! Because of the death you merited the Son of God had to die! And yet you think of nothing but covering your tunics with ornaments (*De Culto Feminarum* I,I in *PL*, I, cols. 304-5).

Clement of Alexandria (c.150–220) writing in a similar vein declared that:

> Nothing disgraceful is proper for man, who is endowed with reason; much less for woman, to whom it brings shame even to reflect what nature she is… By no manner of means are women to be allowed to uncover and exhibit any part of their person, lest both fall—the men by being excited to look, they by drawing on themselves the eyes of men (The writings of Clement of Alexandria as cited in Roberts and Donaldson 1897: 209).

These two quotations demonstrate several important aspects of men's assessment of women's sin which are endemic in the Christian tradition and in derivative social attitudes. The story of the Fall, of Adam and Eve in Gen. 3, is interpreted in such a way as to throw the blame on Eve, making women more culpable than men by their very nature. This culpability is connected with cunning wiles, 'coaxing' and the capacity for sexual manipulation. Woman as sexual temptress is foregrounded in the quotation from Clement; here men's sexual excitement and lack of control is implicitly blamed on (and even projected onto) women, and explicitly used as a means of controlling how women are to dress and deport themselves. It is assumed that when women allow any part of their person to be uncovered it is for the (presumably successful) purposes of attracting men to sexual sin. Furthermore, woman is seen as flippant and irresponsible, concerned primarily with self-adornment, and lacking in reason. Woman is blamed for the shattering of the image of God in 'man' and for the death of Christ.

There is a process at work in what is happening here. It is assumed by the male that he is in possession of reason and is in control. Male experience of sexual lack of control is explained by projecting onto the female the blame for this, which is then given a religious justification in the story of Adam and Eve. This evaluation of woman then goes further into scapegoating her for the presence of evil in the world. This process is shown here in its Christian form. The evaluation of women as source of sexual sin, as possessing less reason and capacity for responsibility than men, and as needing to be controlled, is widespread historically and geographically. Here it is mapped onto Christian theological themes in a way which shapes subsequent thought and action down to the present day.

If a woman's sin is thus defined then the corresponding salvation must lie either in the transcending of her sexuality in a life of purity and virginity, or in chaste submission to her husband who will both control and care for her. This connection is paradigmatically spelt out in the New Testament:

> For Adam was formed first, then Eve; and Adam was not deceived, but the woman was deceived and became a transgressor. Yet she will be saved through childbearing, provided they continue in faith and love and holiness, with modesty (1 Tim. 2. 13-15).

> Do not adorn yourselves outwardly. Rather let your adornment be the inner self with the lasting beauty of a gentle and quiet spirit… It was in this way long ago that the holy women who hoped in God used to adorn themselves by accepting the authority of their husbands. Thus Sarah obeyed Abraham and called him lord. You have become her daughters as long as you do what is good and never let fears alarm you (1 Pet. 3.3-6).

Here it is stated that women should find their salvation as married women in proper obedience to and under the protection of their husbands. While this has been the dominant Protestant view, with Luther emphasizing women's submission as punishment and Calvin emphasizing it as part of the proper social ordering in this world (Douglass 1991), there is also a tradition going back to the New Testament of the *transcending* of sexuality in virginity. A virgin woman transcended her sexuality by becoming *vir* or 'man'; the early legend of

Thecla, a woman who renounced sexual union and sought to become a co-worker with Paul, 'enjoyed great popularity in the early Church, even among the Orthodox' (Armstrong 1990: 83). Historically this tradition can be seen in women's celibate religious orders. While such practices may allow women to lead lives independent of men, and thus be a way of avoiding some of the shackles of patriarchy, the language of obedience to God, of being the 'bride of Christ', stands in place of the language of obedience to men. There is a certain freedom in being directly obedient to God, but in a church context where men have the institutional power, and where those same men seek to identify the will of God with the dictates of the official church, that distinction is somewhat eroded. This complex relationship to authority can be seen in the lives and writings of some of the mediaeval women mystics, who had little or no direct institutional authority, but engaged a different kind of power and authority through their language, their bodily practices and their claims to unmediated mystical experience and revelation (Regnier-Bohler 1992).

It is significant that a key figure, the Virgin Mary, is held up for honour as both perfect mother and perfect virgin. The case of Mary interestingly points up the sense in which purity and virginity may be linked not to the transcendence of the need to obey male authority but to submission and receptivity (as in the annunciation story). C.S. Lewis wrote in his fictional work *That Hideous Strength* that a woman has only two choices, to be a virgin or a Christian wife. In the first case she obeys God directly, in the second, she learns to obey God by obeying her husband.

Submission and receptivity are still seen as key characteristics of the female in particular. Such characteristics are inextricably linked with sexuality, and they are used in the theological rationale for excluding women from priesthood in the Roman Catholic and Orthodox Churches today. This is still the case despite an acceptance that women are made fully in the image of God. In earlier times in Western theology such exclusion of women was based on a belief that they did not in their nature exhibit the rationality necessary for leadership in human or spiritual affairs.[1]

It is noteworthy that both ways to salvation for women outlined above (virginity and Christian marriage/motherhood) are related to sexual and bodily roles. The traditions described, which in various forms dominate the history of the church, give certain answers to the question about what it means to live faithfully as a sexual and embodied woman. But they are answers derived from

---

1.   See Martin (1994) and Ruether (1991) for contrasting Roman Catholic views; Behr-Sigel and Ware (2000) for a discussion of various Orthodox perspectives.

the experiences, the wants and the needs of men, and predicated on an outcome which will bolster male control of a patriarchal system.

A 'Feminine' View

> I am a student of theology; I am also a woman. Perhaps it strikes you as curious that I put these two assertions side by side, as if to imply that one's sexual identity has some bearing on his [*sic*] theological views (Saiving 1995: 3).

So began Valerie Saiving her article 'The Human Situation: A Feminine View', originally published in 1960—an article which has been deeply influential on later feminist theology. In setting out to criticize the prevailing Protestant orthodoxy concerning human sin and salvation, as advocated in particular by Anders Nygren and Reinhold Neibuhr, Saiving took the radical step of asking the gender question: how does their theology make sense in terms of women's experiences? Saiving describes this as *feminine* experience, and a contemporary reader will be struck not only by her automatic use of the generic masculine to describe herself, but also by her somewhat uncritical espousal of certain characteristics as 'feminine'. This should in no way detract from the importance of the step she takes for feminist theology, which is to open up what sin might mean and what salvation might mean for women, *and to claim that they have been wrongly or partially described by men*. Her work addresses both the issues I want to highlight—how concepts of sin and salvation are dialectically related, and how important it is that men *alone* should not define what sin and salvation are, particularly when it is women's sin and women's salvation which are being defined:

Saiving's argument is this. Sin has been defined as pride, the attempt to be like God. Love, sin's opposite, has been defined as self-giving and self-sacrifice. It should be noted that although Saiving is making a detailed critique of a particular, contextually specific theology, the general definition of sin as pride and love as self-giving is widespread in Christian thinking. But women's sin, Saiving argues, is not pride, since women often have too *little* self-esteem and self-regard:

> For the temptations of woman *as woman* are not the same as the temptations of man *as man*, and the specifically feminine forms of sin—'feminine' not because they are confined to women or because women are incapable of sinning in other ways but because they are outgrowths of the basic feminine character structure— have a quality which can never be encompassed by such terms as 'pride' and 'will-to-power'. They are rather suggested by such items as triviality, distractibility, and diffuseness; lack of an organizing center or focus; dependence on others for one's own self-definition; tolerance at the expense of standards of excellence;

inability to respect the boundaries of privacy; sentimentality, gossipy sociability, and mistrust of reason—in short, underdevelopment or negation of the self (Saiving 1995: 13-14).

It is not clear whether this 'basic feminine character structure' arises from biological factors, cultural factors, or a complex interaction of both, and Saiving's actual description of this 'feminine character structure' is undoubtedly culturally specific. Nevertheless, the recognition that negation of the self, far from being a virtue may be a perpetuation of sin, is fundamentally important. The implications for pastoral care of women, as well as for pastoral theological reflection, are revolutionary. This insight is clearly of specific significance in the understanding and care of abused women, but it extends to women's lives in general (Gill-Austern 1996; Bennett Moore 1998a; McFadyen 2000).

Saiving's analysis is a long way from the tradition of blaming women for the sin of Eve (and the sexual sins of men) and of projecting onto women from the viewpoint of men a need to be redeemed through sexual abstinence or motherhood and marital obedience. It is interesting, however, to note that her empirical evaluation of women as at times trivial, distractable, mistrustful of reason and dependent, bears a certain similarity to the description of women as distracted by ornaments, not possessing reason and being dependent on a husband. Of course her wider view is quite different. She implies that such behaviour has been inculcated in women by their social context and conditioning. Her stated purpose is to open the eyes of men and women to the fact that in her own society (1960s, USA) it was becoming possible for women to escape the trap of a lifestyle which encouraged these aspects of character, and to move into new forms of creative cultural fulfilment. But contemporary theological discourse was not enabling this movement. If theologians persist in requiring self-denial from women, and naming the fulfilment of self as sinful pride, then, she suggests:

> [p]erhaps the goal we should set ourselves is to rear our daughters in the older way, without too much formal education and without encouraging them to be independent, differentiated, free human beings of whom some contribution is expected other than the production of the next generation. If we could do this, our daughters might be able to find secure fulfilment in a simple femininity (Saiving 1995: 15).

A Feminist View

Although Saiving calls her article 'a *feminine* view' she incorporates within it the features of a *feminist* analysis. A feminist analysis understands the meaning of sin and salvation in terms of social as well as individual factors ('the personal is political') and is thus concerned ultimately with communal hope for humankind. Saiving asks for a reconsideration of theology's 'estimate of the human condition' and a redefinition of 'its categories of sin and redemption' and ties this closely to the question of what kind of society we propose to build. In what lies the 'salvation' which women should expect and work for? She sees acutely the dilemma which will attend girls brought up in a world of educational opportunity and possibilities for independence, who at the same time are inculturated into a world (particularly, but not only, a *religious* world) dominated by traditions of marriage and submissiveness. Such issues of practice raise the question of whether and how the theological and cultural construction of what it means to be a woman may be changed. They require a renewed understanding of what sin and salvation might mean for women.

Sin. Feminists are divided on the question of whether 'the feminine' is a helpful concept, and if it is, how it should be defined, and whether its features arise biologically or culturally. These difficulties dog any discussion such as Saiving's, where it is necessary for pragmatic reasons to identify certain factors with women's lives, bodies or behaviour. If it is empirically the case that women often display certain traits, such as those Saiving assesses theologically as sin, then have these been brought into being by the very patriarchal structures of society, which have pushed women into these behaviour patterns? If it is so (and she implies it is) it may be better to use the concepts of being 'sinned against' and of 'structural sin' as used in liberation theology, rather than to operate exclusively with a notion of personal sin. Any feminist analysis of what sin means for women must employ these structural categories, as the all-pervasive influence of patriarchy is at the root of so much of the sin experienced by women, objectively and subjectively—'a woman's battered body is the visible mark of the structural sin of a patriarchal society' (Tamez 2001). Use of the language of sin and guilt in relation to abused women highlights this issue of the interconnections between personal and structural sin. 'Dependence on others for one's own self-definition', 'inability to respect the boundaries of privacy', 'underdevelopment or negation of the self' are all according to Saiving characteristics of the 'specifically feminine forms of sin'. These factors feature strongly in many instances of abuse against women and girls. Can it ever be appropriate, and if so how, to use the language of 'sin' here?[2] Alistair McFadyen, in his fascinating discussion of the ways in which the

---

2.   Stephen Pattison in his book *Shame: Theory, Therapy, Theology* (2000) argues for the experiential and theological importance of the category 'shame', which has so often been hidden behind 'sin' and 'guilt' in the Christian tradition. This work is extremely important for a feminist pastoral theological understanding of abuse and its after effects.

feminist theological accounts of sin may illuminate understanding of abuse (McFadyen 2000), refers to the sin Saiving names as 'sloth' and examines how a true reading of the feminist theological position requires a radically new account of the connections between 'sin' and 'culpability', between 'autonomy' and 'intentionality'. Sloth indicates:

> three aspects of the embedded situatedness of persons, and therefore of their willing. It points first to the constriction of the field of possibilities by narrowing down the range of available choices in a gendered way. Second, it suggests that all choosing is caught up in the field of force exerted by the broader material, social and cultural dynamics of 'patriarchy' and finally it indicates that patriarchy has already so embedded itself in internal personhood that its values have become part of a total disorientation of the whole person and her will (McFadyen 2000: 149).

I began this chapter with a reference to the 'myth of feminine evil and the myth of feminine purity'. I have spent some time exposing the myth of feminine evil. The myth of feminine purity may be equally pernicious. In its form of idealized femininity projected by men it takes no account of real women: 'The fact that mother had sexual intercourse with father was the secret scandal of every Victorian household' (Ruether 1975: 21). It may also take a form projected by women—that is the assumption that in a world of women all would be well. This takes equally little account of the lives of real women, as Angela West demonstrates in her exploration of the tensions among the community of women who camped for peace at Greenham Common (West 1995). What West alerts us to here is the importance of remembering the interplay between all factors of oppression (race here as well as sex). Most importantly she urges upon us the importance of attending to real women in the real world, to a realistic assessment of sin and salvation, of evil and goodness as they are made manifest in women's actual lives, not to some idealized or demonized projections.

While an understanding of the violent and distorting nature of the structures in which we live is vital, as is an understanding of the extent to which women are a primary category of the 'sinned against' in patriarchal societies, it is also important for feminist pastoral theology to give some account of both personal sin, and of women as perpetrators of sin. A notion of 'personal sin' which implies that a person acts in a capacity isolated from considerations of societal structure, history or communal values makes very little sense. However, if 'personal sin' refers to the necessity for individuals to take significant responsibility for their own actions, and to recognize themselves as accountable agents, then such a concept would appear to accord well with the emphasis of feminist pastoral theology on the need for women to develop self-identity and subject-quality (Bons-Storm 1996). As for women as perpetrators of sin, our growing understanding of violence in lesbian relationships and of abuse of children by women suggests that power, dominance and physical violence are realities for women as *agents* not just as sufferers. Furthermore, a range of feminist theologians (womanist, Asian, African) have pointed out just how racist white Western women (including feminist theologians) have been (Thistlethwaite 1990; Kwok 2000). The myth of feminine purity encourages blindness to reality just as much as the myth of feminine evil does.

Salvation. As has been seen in relation to traditional views, there is a direct correlation between what is seen as sin and what is seen as salvation. The features of sin from the point of view of women's experience which appear in the above feminist analysis are: embeddedness in sinful ideological and social constructs (i.e. in acting out a destructive 'femininity'); the experience of being sinned against; the refusal or inability to take personal responsibility as an accountable agent; and the perpetration of patterns of violence or exclusion. The corresponding 'salvation' lies in the overcoming of these features.

The first feature of salvation for women on this account is therefore precisely the understanding of the ideological distortions under which we live. 'Conscientization', the coming to a realistic perception of the factors which govern our lives, is itself from this perspective part of the work of salvation.

Second, an understanding of the category 'sinned against' indicates that in order for women to experience salvation we must attend to and resist those things which harm and destroy the lives of women. It is in relation particularly to these two features of women's salvation that I have written this book. My intention is that it should be a contribution to raising awareness among practitioners and students of pastoral theology of those beliefs and practices in the Christian tradition and the Christian churches which are harmful to women, and which go unchallenged because we either do not want to know or do not want to understand.

The third feature of salvation as a correlate of the sin which appears in a feminist analysis is agency, women's agency. A key theme of feminist pastoral theology has been the understanding of women as pastoral agents (Graham 1996) and the development of women's identity and the recognition of women as responsible and truthful subjects (Bons-Storm 1996). This work of salvation requires an intellectual attention to the ways in which knowledge and agency are constructed in our societies and churches. It requires a *practical* commitment to patterns of living which take women's stories seriously, which value women's actions and activities, which welcome women as equal in leadership with men and which honour women's strength. Within this context of responsibility and agency women may, and indeed must, recognise, take responsibility for, and seek to change their own actions which damage and violate others.

Single or Dual Anthropology?

[W]oman seems to be a somewhat different sort of being from man (Luther, quoted in Douglass 1991: 242).

Hence there are two utterly distinct and original ways of being a human person (Martin 1994: 991).

Luther identifies what makes a women different from a man in terms of both her body and her nature (*ingenium*). This understanding of difference underwrites his assertions about the proper role of a woman as a wife and mother. Francis Martin, explicating the teaching of Pope John Paul II (1981), argues for a strong view of the complementarity and the bipolarity of the sexes, rooted in a relational understanding of the Trinity. He quotes the Pope: 'the knowledge of man passes through masculinity and femininity, which are, as it were, two "incarnations" of the same metaphysical solitude, before God and the world—two ways, as it were, of "being a body" and at the same time a man' (1981: 79). This understanding of difference underwrites Martin's assertions about the role of heterosexual marriage and the exclusion of women from the priesthood.

It can thus be seen, in two quite different ecclesial and social contexts, how an understanding of 'woman' as radically different from 'man' may be used in the service of a complementarity that masks domination. Some feminists, therefore, have sought to play down the dualism of man/woman and to bring out the similarities of men and women in their common humanity. Others, however, have emphasized the differences and used them for feminist ends. Before examining these strategies more closely I intend to widen the perspective a little.

What is it to be Human?

It would appear to be natural for people to assume that they are normal and that everyone else is not. This appears in forms ranging from the personal (my mother's oft repeated dictum that 'no one's sane except you and me—and I'm not so sure about you sometimes') to the national and global (the classical Greek description of those who were not Greeks as 'barbarians'—they could not speak Greek but gabbled 'bar-bar'). Such concepts have gradually been overcome in Western theoretical thought as, since the eighteenth century, we have gained an increasing understanding of how in different historical periods and different cultural contexts what is considered 'normal' and 'rational' and 'good' differs radically. Postmodernism has brought an increased and more complex under-standing of these differences. It is arguable however that theoretical thinking and practice have not kept in step, as colonization and oppression and demoni-zation of those who are 'other' have continued throughout this period.

This understanding of human particularity and of the significance of differ-ence has posed questions for pastoral theology and practice. For example, it has raised questions about how women may be represented by a male Christ, and it has thrown into doubt whether men can empathize with women (Bons-Storm 1996) or people from one culture with people from another (Lartey 1997). The question of what may be considered as common humanity is a vexed one. But it is a matter of life-and-death importance, as the entitlement to human rights is often seen to rest on an acceptance of common humanity. To refer to a sick person as a vegetable, or to an enemy as an animal, is the discourse which legitimates killing them.

Lewis Mudge draws attention not only to the changing character of how we see common humanity, but also crucially to our *agency*, and our possibilities for shaping that perspective and that reality. He writes:

> Our grasp of the meaning of humanity depends today on discerning the changing, perhaps disintegrating, character of the human world of which we are a part, in which we play our roles. By our relationships and deeds we are actively forming our reality even as we seek to find categories for grasping it… The very meaningfulness of 'humanity' as a comprehensive category thus rests on con-tingent historical developments (Mudge 1999: 29).

Pastoral theology may shape as well as note what is the case. Bons-Storm and Lartey not only note the difficulties of trans-gender and trans-cultural empathy, but they also assert possibilities and explore ways of making these real.

The question of what it means to be human is thus about human relation-ships. It is also about seeing the human in its wider context. This must include the rest of the created order—what has traditionally been described as 'nature'—and refuse a false isolation of humanity from the rest of the natural world (Grey 1989: ch. 3; Clinebell 2000). On the other hand, what it is to be human must be understood today in connection with the 'artificial' world of machines, body implants, digital and medical technology and genetic engineering (Graham 2001).

'Lady's and Normal'
The question of the differentiation between men and women is one question within this wider context. It has of course deep connections with all the factors

mentioned above: the use of difference to devalue, oppress and caricature, the difficulty of understanding across difference, the situation of fluidity and change which calls for proactive involvement, the embeddedness in bodily reality and nature, the effects of new technologies. Man/woman, the gender dualism, is one particular concept within this overall picture. It can be approached historically and empirically—have women's lives in history and today actually been so radically different from men's lives that we have in effect a dual anthropology—'two ways of being human'? The question can be approached biologically—are women and men 'different sorts of beings' with different capabilities? It can be approached normatively and theologically—are men and women created differently and meant for different roles by God?

The problem with any of these approaches comes when one side of the dualism is taken as normal, or as the norm. This is what happens in popular speech, when the man in the outdoor pursuits shop repeated the ingrained assumption that men's body size constituted the norm—'one lady's, one normal'. It happens in religious thinking. A student in a seminar I was leading gave the opinion that when he thought of God as male there were no sexual overtones, but when he thought of God as female the image became sexualized and difficult. I think he speaks honestly for many of us, men and women, because 'male' is somehow just 'normal' in our consciousness whereas 'female' is 'sex'-specific as well as gender-specific. As feminist theologians have attempted to balance the androcentric bias of the way the Christian tradition has been lived and expressed they have placed women in the foreground. But there is a constant danger of women appearing as something abnormal or something additional to the male norm. Saiving's discussion of women's sin is not meant to add an interesting extra dimension to an otherwise unchanged norm; it is meant to correct the whole doctrine of sin. In commenting on Saiving's thesis William Cahoy points out:

> Male experience has been made normative and women's experience, to the extent that it has been acknowledged as different, is defined as 'the other' requiring separate study and explanation. But women are, after all, human. Hence, the point of the feminist critique is not simply that the traditional analysis is untrue to *women's* experience but that it is untrue to *human* experience (Cahoy 1995: 431).

In biblical and historical study women are written *about*. That Paul's attitude to women should be discussed is important, but women here are still the objects, not the subjects—what about women's attitude to Paul? Of course, historically speaking, access to women's views is not always as easy to gain as access to men's. Women, in Bernadette Brooten's image, are often viewed somewhat like clay figurines. Within the framework of history which is set up women are:

> subsumed under such categories as 'the role of women', or 'the status of women'. Such terminology evokes the image of the landscape of male reality that is varied and complex... Into this dynamic and active landscape, we now place woman, a clay figurine, which is put into place at some one point on the moving scene. One can now discuss her role, her status, her relation to men on the scene (Brooten 1985: 82-83).

Brooten's model discloses to us the importance of going beyond the *discussion about* women to putting women at the *centre of the stage as subjects*. She uses the analogy to explore what must be done in terms of historical study to allow women to speak as subjects, and indeed to expose how difficult that task is.

This discussion illustrates two points which must be made in the consideration of single or dual anthropology. First, both the actual history of women and the writing of women's history have been very different from male experience. Women's history is often read between the lines of male-authored history. Second, the male experience is viewed as normative—the position from which to view; while the female is viewed as 'other' and as that which is to be viewed. If *human* experience is to be explored then ways must be found of facilitating the conversation between very different male and female experiences 'without making either one normative for the other' (Cahoy 1995: 447). This applies equally to experiences of everyday life, to the vision of God and to our understanding of the past.

Feminist Anthropology
Feminists have responded in a variety of ways to the question of how gender specificity is related to generic 'humanness' (see Carr 1988: 117-33; Ruether 1983: 102-115; 1991: 284-86). Some, primarily liberal feminists, have emphasized that both men and women are first and foremost human and that to all intents and purposes gifts, abilities, rights and responsibilities are not shared among people according to a gender division. Others have emphasized the specific characteristics of women (whether acquired by nature or by nurture) but, rather than using this distinctiveness to cast women as subordinate or excluded from certain roles, have pointed out how full human living needs the contributions of both men and women. This is, for example, how many have argued for the inclusion of women in the pastorate and priesthood. Yet others (radical or romantic feminists) have asserted the superiority of what women are over what men are, some such as Mary Daly going as far as to advocate separatist strategies for living. All this must be seen in a context in which the 'human' is not a fixed but a fluid concept, and the representation of 'the human' is subject both to ideological construction and to imaginative re-envisioning.

Reality and Vision

Dual anthropology has been the material condition under which we have lived, and it is still our experience. Biology, culture and experience are part of what make up our very selves, and at this level men's and women's experiences are often radically different. Women's situation of cultural inferiority is observed as universal (Ortner 1995). It is inappropriate to speak theologically of a single anthropology while ignoring the real and painful differences which sex and gender impose at the deepest level on real lives. But this dual condition is not unalterable. Social actualities and cultural views reproduce one another, but there is room for intervention in either of these and such intervention in one will affect the other. Dual anthropology exists in fact in our actual lives, but it is not necessarily the condition under which we are bound to live.

Single anthropology, on the other hand, has been used as an idealist projection. The assertion that women and men are equal before God, equal in salvation and of equal worth has served to cover up materially unjust and sinful conditions for women. This happens because women are said to have different roles from men. It is men who are to be leaders, heads of the household and priests. The response of feminist theologians to this situation varies. Some emphasize the inadequacy of taking the male norm as that to which women should aspire—asking Luce Iragary's question, 'equal to whom?' (Parsons 2000a: 12) Others emphasize strongly the need to work for justice, in a way which utilizes the goal of equality, while also indicating that our view of what is it to be human should not be based on a male perspective; women do not just want to be 'honorary men'. Rosemary Radford Ruether writes of a single or unitary anthropology as an 'expanded unitary view of human nature, possessed fully and equally by men and women' (1991: 286), including both traditionally male capacities and traditionally female capacities. Such a view must continue to highlight the way in which actual historical conditions militate against the achievement of this in lived reality.

There is here an instructive analogy with women's utopian writing. Feminist utopia is sometimes envisaged as a world in which men and women are equal, sometimes as a world in which men are excluded, and sometimes as a world in which sex roles are reversed. Christian feminist eschatological vision needs to embrace a full and equal humanity for both men and women, as in the first of these; such a vision should act as a thorn in the side of the present reality. But the notions of equality and especially of complementarity, however good and plausible they sound in theory, have in Christian history often legitimated an oppressive reality. So some feminists have found utopia in a separatist vision.

However, it may be that imaginative envisaging and actual engagement with something more like a sex-role-reversal utopia would cut most deeply into our present reality and disturb us more creatively.[3] One of my most creative memories of school English lessons was the year an imaginative (and not in the least feminist) teacher invited us (a class of girls) to rewrite and enact Act 3 of *Hamlet* with the sex-roles reversed. A similar exercise, if conducted at a level beyond the superficial, would in most churches be revolutionary.

A Woman in the Image of God?

I return to Gen. 1.27. Although the third part of the verse 'male and female he created them' may not imply anything in its original context about *sexuality* in God, the text as a whole is used and rightly used as an inclusive statement that all human beings are made in the image of God. 'Thus it may serve as a foundation text for a feminist egalitarian anthropology, since it recognises no hierarchy of gender in the created order' (Bird 1991: 19). This text has indeed served as a symbol of that equality for all people, which founds their claim to human rights. To name oneself made in the image of God is to claim equal value with other human beings; it means to claim the human right to be free of violence or the threat of violence. This is part of what it means to live as a sexual and embodied human being.

There are at least three significant theological starting points in which to locate the claim to be made in the image of God, as I outlined at the beginning of Chapter 4. The first is creation, which is the Gen. 1 starting point. Women's value is rooted in their creation equally with men in the image of God. The second starting point is with Christology. Jesus Christ is seen as the image of God. Those who follow Christ, men and women, are called to the 'imitation of Christ', both personally and as part of the 'christic community'. Such imitation has to do with a life of love, compassion and 'action on behalf of those whose basic human dignity has been violated' (Hilkert 1995: 202). The third starting point is in eschatology: the self is being renewed according to the image of its creator.

Eschatology is a problematic concept for feminists. This is because of the desire to emphasize a life-loving attitude to the present rather than a long-range pietistic vision which ignores both the joys and the injustices of the present. It is also because eschatology has so often been used to say women are equal in heaven but subordinate on earth, or to distract from present injustice

---

3.   I am grateful to my daughter Naomi Humphries, for these insights into feminist sex-role-reversal utopias (see Humphries 2001).

by the hope of future fulfilment. Nevertheless, it seems to me that to root women's full humanity in that to which they are called as both promise and as task is to take realistic account of the painful experiences of the present while at the same time saying, 'it does not have to be like this'. Such an emphasis on task and on future hope also invites both a commitment to justice and equality *and* a questioning of precisely to what or to whom women are to be equal. Human nature in the image of God is for both men and women a calling as much as something given. Such a calling is part of what it means to live faithfully as a sexual and embodied human being. As women and men wrestle in society, in church and in private relationships with new ways of relating, a vision of the future in the loving intention of God acts as the religious version of theory: 'it *will not* always be like this'.

Chapter Six

A Community in the Image of God

This chapter is both a bridge and a pivot. As a bridge it has one foot in the issues of the previous chapters—the violence which structures so much of men's and women's experience of life, the Bible and the Christian tradition, human understanding of God and of what it is to be a human person. The other foot of the bridge is in the following chapter—on women and pastoral care. This bridging chapter is about the church, about that community which understands itself to be the body of Christ, growing together into the image of God. The church is the most difficult aspect of Christianity for most feminists.[1] Despite this, the church is the context, more or less immediate, for Christian pastoral care. In the church we find the sharp end of all the practical and theological difficulties encountered in this book. And so consideration of the church is not only a bridge within this book, it is also a pivot. I remember once asking as a theology student why it should be the case that belief in the trinitarian Christian God should depend upon the possibility of there being at least somewhere a place where the love of God is seen in human community. My professor asked me what I would think of a God who claimed to be a creator but who hadn't created anything. We claim that God loves the created world, desires a relationship with humankind and is in God's very self a 'community of persons'. 'No one has ever seen God; if we love one another, God lives in us, and his love is perfected in us' (Jn 4.12). The community in which the love of God is manifested is the community in which there is hope in the face of all the distortions of violence, of language, of injustice, of faith and of theology. It is the community in which, however haltingly and imperfectly, pastoral care may be given and received.

It is not, therefore, an accident that the WCC Decade of the Churches in

---

1.   And this is not only true for feminists—Franz Overbeck said 'the best school for learning to doubt the existence of God as ruler of the world is church history' (quoted in Barth 1962: 61).

Solidarity with Women found violence to be a key issue for the church. Violence in all its forms prevents faithful and authentic community. The Ecumenical Decade named violence as a sin, and demonstrated that the question of violence in the churches is not only a question of justice for women, it is also a question of ecclesiology. It is about the way power and authority are exercised in church structures. 'The Decade ended with women speaking of their longing for the realization of a more authentic and more faithful community of women and men in the church—but also, and too often, with silence from the churches' (Gnanadason 2001: 2). In so much of the church there is still silence concerning 'the male power which lies at the heart of so many church structures, and ... the violence and oppression which many women experience within the institutional churches' (Crawford 2001: 22). As has been seen in the preceding chapters, this violence, or violation, is not just manifest in the practices of church communities, but also in the beliefs and language that underlie and reinscribe those practices. This chapter will, therefore, examine various aspects of what it means to be a community that seeks to make visible and real the love of God and to be the body of Christ to the world.

I have written already of the feminist theology course in which four men and I wrote what we called a 'midrash'. This was a piece of creative writing based on a biblical passage, the great banquet of Lk. 14 (Bennett Moore 1998b). I propose to use this story to highlight the various aspects of the church I wish to examine.

The story begins with Pastor Matthew, the Reverend Mark, Father Luke and John Johnson, former Moderator of an unnamed church General Assembly, arriving at a sumptuous feast in a splendid hall, guests of a hostess about whom we know little except that she is associated with wisdom.

> The room was large and warm. High oak-panelled walls reached up to the intricately-plastered ceiling. The candles on the table blazed merrily and the food glistened in opulent splendour. The gentlemen sat at a table which creaked under the weight of such an enormous feast.

The churchmen are totally engrossed in eating and drinking and talking, although their hunger and thirst increase:

> And Pastor Matthew ate and looked on.
> And the Reverend Mark ate and was served some more.
> And Father Luke ate and ate again.
> And John Johnson talked and ate, and ate and talked.

They don't notice as gradually more and more people fill the room—refugees, women and children, prostitutes, poor and colonized people, homeless and sick people. They continue to be self-engrossed as they eat and talk on.

The room began to heave. People seeped in through the windows and poured through the doors. The gentlemen didn't even stir when the plaster fell from the ceiling and even more folk were lowered through the roof. People, glistening with sweat, pressed down upon the diners.

The men began to mutter and complain.

Pastor Matthew looked up.
Father Luke stopped eating.
John Johnson was silent.
And no-one served the Reverend Mark.

And the crowds pressed harder still. It felt as though nobody could move a muscle in the tense and teeming heat.

They called upon the hostess: 'Mary, how can we eat?' Stepping forward she heaved the table over and scattered the food. Turning on the men she exclaimed, 'You have turned my home into a den of gluttons!'

In silence everyone's gaze rested upon the nail-marks in her hands.

'Sit' she said. And an old woman took from the food scattered on the floor a loaf of bread. Breaking it she said, 'Take, eat, for we are all invited'. Slowly the food was passed from person to person and all ate their fill.

And as they shared in the feast
Pastor Matthew saw and understood.
The Reverend Mark served his neighbour and was glad.
Father Luke rested and was satisfied.
And John Johnson listened.

Aruna Gnanadason, in writing of the way forward after the Ecumenical Decade, identifies four theological themes to be explored in the engagement with women's voices and visions, as the church worldwide seeks for renewal and greater unity (Gnanadason 2001: 2-3). These are: metaphors and models of the church—old and new; word, sacrament and liturgy; community diversity and justice; partnership and the exercise of power. All of these themes are clearly present in the 'midrash'.

Metaphors and Models of the Church—Old and New

Our 'midrash' presented a model of the church that arose directly from our particular struggle with our own church and context in Cambridge, our understanding of the Bible and Christian tradition, and our wrestling with the challenges, often deeply personal and convicting, of feminist theology—remember four of us were men. The 'church' we depicted is experiencing deep and painful change, indeed almost breaking up and caving in. But it is a church in which there is ultimate hope—hope for the salvation of both women and men. It is an inclusive church. Its visual symbols are the overturning of tables and the sharing of food.

Within feminist theology such themes recur. Elisabeth Schüssler Fiorenza, writing in 1990 of the vision of Vatican II and lamenting the suppression of that vision, speaks of the *discipleship of equals*: 'Through the conciliar process the discipleship of equals has been incarnated as a lived reality among the people of God. Women have emerged as creative, articulate and trail-blazing members in the church and in its ministry' (Schüssler Fiorenza 1993a: 293).

Fiorenza in her historical work finds this community of equals in the early Christian vision of the *basileia* ('reign') of God (1983). She and other feminist writers regularly use the word *ekklesia* to denote church, but to indicate a quite different vision of church from the patriarchal norm; her vision is of a community where all are understood to be called equally by God, where the gifts of all flourish, and where love, care and respect are accorded to all. Other popular feminist metaphors of the church relate to roundness and circles—the 'roundtable', the 'circle' the 'church in the round' (Russell 1993). The point here is equality in speaking, in decision making and in status. The circle is also about sharing food at table with none more privileged than the other, and about dance, and about facing others in full openness. A similar vision is behind the African women's image of church as 'God's household' (Oduyoye 2001b: 46). This is an organic image, which invites questions about the relationships between those in the household and the way its members are valued. Letty Russell explores the image of 'sanctuary' for the church, 'a place of safety for all who enter, and especially for those who are the most marginal, weak or despised of any community' (Russell 2001: 48).

All these various metaphors for the church emerge from experiences or visions of those, here particularly women, struggling to be God's people. One particular issue arises for feminists—what place is there for women-only church gatherings, or for gatherings of women and men who actively support the feminist cause? A range of such projects is described in *On Being Church: Women's Voices and Visions* (WCC 2001), including Women Church in Korea, The St Hilda Community in Britain and *Con-spirando* in Latin America. The term 'women church' is often (though not always) used to identify such groups, which may or may not include men. The term 'has been used in the US and elsewhere since 1983 and does not refer to a separate denomination, but rather to ecumenical groups who gather for inclusive liturgy, support, advocacy for change, and development of inclusive spirituality' (Russell 2001: 55). Sometimes the felt need for such groups is specific, for example the formation of the St Hilda Community arose from the struggle for women to become priests in the Church of England. At other times it is related to a desire to be more inclusive, or more politically committed, than is possible within the authority structures and life-patterns of existing denominations and traditions. Or the motivation may centre round the way worship and liturgy take place.

It has been argued that it is necessary for women to meet together, and separately from men, *for the time being*, perhaps on an occasional basis, in order to begin to find the strength and support necessary for the struggle to reform the churches, or perhaps even the struggle to stay in them.

> Distressing as it may seem to males who imagine themselves sympathetic to feminism, this process of consciousness raising must necessarily have a separatist stage. Women have to withdraw from male-dominated spheres so they can gather together and define their own experience... [W]e are not talking here about separatism as total ideology, but as a stage in a process, a stage that is absolutely necessary but not an end in itself, a stage toward a further end in the formation of a critical culture and community of women and men in exodus from patriarchy (Ruether 1985b: 59-60).

This is often, however, seen as divisiveness, and fiercely resisted. Furthermore, since the issues which cause pain are so often tied to issues of authority and boundary-keeping, for example, women's leadership or presidency at the Eucharist, or worship shared between people of different faiths, then such 'women church' gatherings may attract official disapproval and even persecution for 'disobedience'. The model of the church which emerges from such feminist practices all over the world is one of tension and provisionality and struggle.

It is interesting in this context to reflect on the roles which have been played throughout the history of the church by women-only organizations *within* the official church structures. In recent history we could instance the Mothers' Union, the Catholic Women's League, and the various forms of women's guilds, young wives clubs and so on which abound in churches of all ecclesial traditions. Such organizations may perform a nurturing and supportive role for women, or may provide outlets for women to serve the church and the world. They may indeed empower women to live fuller lives in church and society, but their location within the official frameworks of the churches mean that women's power and authority within them may be carefully circumscribed by theological or cultural factors.[2]

---

2.   For a specifically focused discussion of the role of women's organizations in the Roman Catholic Church in Zambia see Namalambo (2001).

I have concentrated thus far on new metaphors and models for church emerging from women-identified communities and practices. These are, of course, not all entirely new. They may be seen in creative continuity or tension with other metaphors and models—biblical metaphors such as the church as a body or a building (Minear 1961) and theological models such as the church as sacrament, herald or servant (Dulles 1976). A preferred model in recent ecumenical discussions is *koinonia* or communion. This would appear to have potential for inclusivity, but a metaphor does not stand alone, apart from the actions of the communities who use it. It is salutary to note that 'there is little evidence that the theme of koinonia has helped to "heal the wounds of women", or that ecumenical discussion focused on this concept has encouraged the inclusion of women's perspectives on ecclesiology' (Crawford 2001: 21).

One biblical metaphor for the church is particularly problematic in a feminist analysis, that is the image of the church as the bride of Christ. The problem has various roots and various effects, but the central reason that this metaphor has been used to undergird violent patriarchy is that it is based on the marriage relationship—the key man–woman relationship in most human societies—which is itself deeply affected by the violence of patriarchy. The religious concept is distorted by the unequal and often violent human practices. Then in turn the religious concept, so distorted, actually legitimates the very things that are wrong in the human relationships.

The way in which the problems with this image appear varies according to denomination and tradition. In the Orthodox and Roman Catholic communions a supposed connection between the active, giving God and the male human being, in distinction to the receptive female human being, is foundational for the restriction of the priesthood to men. In recent Roman Catholic thought the *nuptial metaphor* for the sexual bipolarity of human bodies has been developed to the point where it underpins a range of theological concepts—Trinity, Christology, ecclesiology (church, sacraments, ministry), anthropology—as well as ethical issues around sexuality and marriage.[3] This view of the human body is inseparable from the nuptial metaphor for the church, and is used to reinforce a notion of complementarity in church life which is so often a mask for male dominance.

In Protestant thinking the parallels between 'God/Christ–church', on the one hand, and 'man–woman' on the other, serve the interests of male headship—that is male leadership in church and in marriage. 1 Corinthians 11,

---

3. Martin (1994: 388-91) following, in which he draws on the work of von Balthasar and Pope John Paul II.

especially v. 3, is key here: 'But I want you to understand that Christ is head of every man, and the husband is head of his wife, and God is the head of Christ.' This, taken together with various passages suggesting a subordinate female role in church contexts, acts as the founding biblical metaphor for women's 'complementary and different' role. The passage in Eph. 5 which begins 'Husbands, love your wives, just as Christ loved the church' certainly enjoins a kind and nurturing relationship from husband to wife, but also engenders precisely the kind of unilateral dependency identified as 'women's sin' in Chapter 5. Although it is clear that the intention of this passage is in no way violent, in practice the complementarity it advocates fosters at best a patronizing attitude from men to women, at worse implicit if not explicit violence.

Word, Sacrament and Liturgy

This is the second theological theme identified by Gnanadason. In the 'midrash' there is a great deal implied about word, sacrament and liturgy, all of which resonates with themes important to feminists. How God is worshipped and how the presence of God is felt and acknowledged are crucial elements of what it means to be a community made in the image of God.

The whole 'midrash' is an imaginative exploration based on a biblical passage. The themes of invitation, of inclusiveness, of surprise, of reversal and of generosity are all already present in Luke's text. The words of the hostess, 'You have turned my home into a den of gluttons' are based on Lk. 19.46. More indirectly the names of the four men and the hostess are all biblical, but used in a way which reverses common understandings. The 'word' is here present, but in a new way.

Sacramentally speaking the story is rich. The denouement is based on the Eucharist. Food is prominent, and eating brings both judgment and blessing. The sacramental role of human beings is clear, in opening eyes and understanding and in mediating the presence of God, by presence or by word. The sacramental blessing is inclusive, 'we are all invited', in a context in which many might expect to be excluded (including by this stage the men). The 'sacramental presidency' is shared and is held by women. The 'Christ role' is indicated by the overturning of the tables, but above all by the nail marks in the hostess's hands. The association of wisdom with the hostess links to the feminist identification of Jesus Christ with the figure of Wisdom/Sophia outlined in Chapter 4. The use of the name Mary is evocative of the roles of the various Marys in the Bible—perhaps, given the reversal theme, especially Mary Magdalene, portrayed in so much of Christian tradition as a weak and needy woman or an evil, sexual sinner. There is a strong sense of disturbance and reversal, as the room becomes overcrowded and then as the tables are over-turned. This mediates a sense of the transcendent, that which is beyond human control or expectation. Finally there is transformation, in the shared meal, and in the new insight and behaviour of the four men.

There are strong liturgical elements in this story. The actual 'liturgy' depicted at the end is both personal and political. It is inextricably embedded in the actual lives and current circumstances of the people taking part. As such it is in its precise form ephemeral and unrepeatable. It involves the unexpected; it involves conversion. People learn to look and to listen, to rest and to share. The liturgy is simple. There are few words, a strong and immediate symbol, action on the part of all (passing the bread) and a clear connection to life and community. The bread, by contrast with the luscious food mentioned earlier, is plain and nutritious, and it is scattered on the floor amid mess and chaos.

In this examination of a particular story some key elements of a feminist approach to worship and liturgy come to light. The feminist liturgist Marjorie Procter-Smith identifies five values that 'give feminist liturgical events a char-acter which is distinctive' (Procter-Smith 1990: 22-25). *Contextuality* is indicated in the specificity of acts of worship to particular occasions; feminist liturgies are often unrepeatable because they are designed for a particular time and place. The year group following the one which wrote the 'midrash' wrote and enacted a liturgical act of worship. The 'midrash' we published; the text of the liturgy we deliberately threw away. *Commitment to process* is shown in the way in which much feminist liturgy arises from a group process in which the creation of the liturgy is as important as the liturgy itself. *Experimentality* describes the creative risk-taking and the acceptance of things being 'on the way' rather than perfected which characterize feminist worship and liturgy. *Explicit rejection of hierarchical forms of liturgical leadership* and *corresponding commitment to shared leadership* are expressed in the maximizing of the participation of all and also in the preference for circular space. Finally, there is a preference for *ecumenicity* in the widest sense of the word. 'In gatherings of women, then, denominational, confessional, or traditional divisions are relativised' (Procter-Smith 1990: 25).

In feminist pastoral theology the area of 'word, sacrament and liturgy' is of supreme importance. Feminist pastoral theology should include an under-standing of contemporary worship and liturgy and how these relate to the pastoral needs and interests of women (Procter-Smith 1990; 1995a), of the history of 'women's ways of worship' (Berger 1999), of the place and inter-pretation of the Bible in worship (Procter-Smith 1993; Winter 1991; 1997) and of the significance of the language of worship (Ramshaw 1995).[4]

---

4.   For an introduction to all these areas under one cover the reader is referred to Janet

Community, Diversity and Justice

> This [theme] demands an investigation of women's perspectives on the work for
> unity and their insights into identity, diversity and community; and reflection on
> ways to energize forces of life, and to overcome violence and other forms of
> injustice in the midst of the groaning of creation (Gnanadason 2001: 3).

This is how Aruna Gnanadason sees the agenda for the continued WCC
exploration of her third theological theme. The 'midrash' places the issue of
justice, with its attendant themes of community and diversity, at the heart of
its understanding of 'church', of what it means to be a community made in the
image of God. Through the presence of the despised and oppressed groups of
people, who are at first ignored, and then resented, and finally utterly transform the community, the theme of just community takes centre stage. The
greed and introverted selfishness of the four men is changed by the actions of
the other guests and of the hostess—actions which have strong christological
and eucharistic overtones. In the inclusion of those previously despised or
rejected, and in the sharing bread together, the forces of life are clearly identified in the diversity of the community,

The themes of community, diversity and justice have appeared throughout
this book, as aspects of feminist pastoral theology. Feminist pastoral theology
is pluralist and dialogical in its approach to understanding truth. Feminist pastoral theologians generally work collaboratively. Mutuality of pastoral care is
emphasized. Feminist liturgy arises from the experiences and understandings
of a community, and that community is often itself diverse.

To speak of diversity is to raise the question of acceptable diversity, the
question of boundaries. Working as I do in a federation of theological institutions from a wide diversity of ecclesial traditions this is an issue which is constantly raised for me. Three points would seem to be important. The first is that
'boundaries' is the wrong image. Much better is an image of a central *commitment* which holds things and people together by attraction to the centre rather
than by a policing of the boundaries.[5] Second, inclusiveness is of itself a gospel
value, and as such of more importance than doctrinal, political or moral correctness. Indeed, commitments to *love* and to grace as primary are themselves
doctrinal, political and moral commitments. Third, vigorous *witness* to our own

Wootton's book in the Introductions in Feminist Theology series, *Introducing a Practical
Feminist Theology of Worship* (2000).

    5.   I am indebted to Letty Russell for this insight at the 'Women and Leadership'
Seminar at Bossey, June 2001.

perspective on the truth does not entail the silencing or exclusion of those with whom we disagree, of those from different social or religious backgrounds, or of those whose own witness is very different. These perspectives, which grow from an ecumenical context of working, are consonant with feminist perspectives. While women make up the vast majority of church membership in many countries, it is also true that women are often externally marginalized from power, decision-making and leadership in the churches. They are also internally marginalized by their inability to make any sense out of their own stories because these don't have any recognisable relationship to the stories told by the churches. A community seeking to reflect the image of God will welcome the stranger and listen to the story which disturb the complacently religious.

What is more, the issue of violence against women, prima facie an issue of justice, has been seen to be fundamentally an issue of ecclesiology. When violence against women happens in the churches, is condoned by the churches and is even fostered by the traditions of the churches, then a fundamental question mark is raised over the claim of the church in general, and churches in particular, to be bearers of the presence of God. This is the case whether this presence of God is viewed congregationally, sacramentally or hierarchically.

So the issue of working for justice and inclusion is not an added extra 'good work' but a fundamental issue of the nature of church and community. For this reason 'women church' and other communities with feminist vision are normally strongly committed to issues, or perhaps one particular issue, of social justice. For example, Sook-Ja Chung writes of Women Church in Korea:

> But Women Church is not only a worshipping community, but also an *action* community involved in social justice issues. Thus Women Church takes the responsibility for leading demonstrations… Women Church often 'displaces' its services of worship, bringing them into the settings of those who are suffering (Chung 2001: 80).

A community made in the image of God sees the sufferings of fellow human beings and offers help. A community made in the image of God will suffer the transformation of its own inner life through attention to its own unjust practices.

Partnership and the Exercise of Power

The 'midrash' illustrates several aspects of a feminist approach to partnership and power in the church. First, the Christ figure is female. As has been seen in the resistance to the 'Christa' figure and also in the resistance in some churches to a woman representing Christ, this is a controversial and resisted image. Second, the 'ministry' in the story is done in partnership—Mary issues the rebuke, overturns the tables and commands people to sit. The old woman takes, breaks and offers the bread. The people, including the Reverend Mark, pass the bread to one another.

Third, it is not insignificant that the one who offers the bread is an old woman. Recently I attended an international conference of women at which a senior theological college teacher introduced her remarks by saying with dignity, 'I am a woman. I am poor. I am black. And I am old.' Old women are so often treated without respect, and indeed may be last in the queue for material resources too.

Fourth, the roles which clearly relate to ministry and priesthood are taken by women, in spite of the titles accorded to the men (Pastor, Reverend, Father, Moderator). At some point in a book on feminist pastoral theology the issue of women and ordination must be tackled. Many feminist women are reluctant to centre on this issue as it may distract from wider issues which have more immediate and pressing relevance to the lives of women. But within the church it is a kind of litmus test. The issues surrounding the ordination of women show up patriarchy in the churches in its true colours.

The WCC Decade of the Churches in Solidarity with Women identified the lack of real partnership between women and men in the churches as a key issue, of which the refusal to allow women to be ordained is an integral part. This refusal is of a piece with more general exclusion and with patronizing, domineering and violent treatment of women. There is a 'constant underlying resistance' (Field-Bibb 1991: 262) to women's ordination, which may take the form of official refusal of ordination, or of the toleration of official dissent from the ordination of women, or of the subtle forms of exclusion which bypass official equal opportunities commitments. Field-Bibb points as evidence for this deep-seated resistance to the way in which the argument against ordination of women in the Church of England slipped between the biblical, the traditional and the symbolic as each one became problematic. Crawford (2001) illustrates the same process in the WCC's Faith and Order Committee in respect of the issue of women's ordination. While it is recognized as a serious issue in the *Baptism, Eucharist and Ministry* text (WCC 1982) and in the responses to that text (WCC 1990a) it has not been taken up and tackled head-on in the way other issues have. The more recent study document *Church and World* (WCC 1990b) gives

> no hint…of the passionate nature of the struggle for the full participation of
> women in the church, nor of the growing tensions which the search for a
> renewed community of women and men was creating, within and between the

member churches of the WCC and in the very structures of the WCC itself (Crawford 2001: 20).

Thus the ordination of women often acts symbolically to bring out the underlying resistance to women's partnership on equal terms in church and ministry. It also appears to call forth manifestations of the kind of implicit and explicit violence against women which I have repeatedly identified as endemic to the patriarchal structure of society and church. This may be illustrated both from a church which tolerates official dissent and discrimination against women (the Church of England) and from a church which does not (the Methodist Church in England). In March 2000 the *Daily Telegraph* reported on a recent study of women priests in the Church of England by Helen Thorne of Bristol University (Thorne 2000):

> Women interviewed for the study…said that they had experienced discrimination ranging from silent protests, such as refusing to take communion from a woman priest, to rare instances of physical sexual assault.
>
> The extent of the problem facing many women priests is shown by statistics which found that a quarter of the respondents claimed to have experienced some form of sexual harrassment.
>
> More than half—57 per cent—said they had been treated rudely by colleagues while 40 per cent said they had 'difficult' relations with bishops or senior clergy…
>
> The report also attacked the 1993 Act of Synod which established 'flying bishops' for parishes that did not recognise the ordination of women. Dr Thorne said that the Act was seen to 'violate and harm women' because it legitimised sexism and 'gives credence to the malicious and malevolent behaviour they have experienced in the church' (*Daily Telegraph* 7 March 2000).

I have quoted this at length because it shows strikingly the seamless robe which connects opposition to the ordination of women, sexual violation, rudeness and malice, and the legitimation of these things in the refusal of the church to outlaw sexual discrimination. These things are cornerstones of the patriarchal violence of the church, and they are legitimated by biblical and theological arguments.

However, all is not rosy in the garden even where the church officially offers equal opportunities. It was reported to the Methodist Conference in Britain in 1995, after 20 years of ordination of women to the presbyteral ministry, that women presbyters identified the following difficulties among others—invisibility, paternalism, stereotyping, jokes that trivialize the issue, personal criticism unrelated to work, the 'we can't have two women in a row' syndrome, games played by male ministers (especially the misuse of power), sexual harrassment (*A Cry of the Beloved* Agenda of Methodist Conference 1995). Once again women exercising ministry call forth the phenomena that are the publicly acceptable face of patriarchy's violence. No community in which such things happen and are tolerated can be said to image God, except of course by the ideological distortion which images God as legitimating sexism.

Pastoral Action and the Christian Community—the Bridge

Resisting, empowering, nurturing and liberating within a communal and contextual understanding of that action—these are the characteristics of pastoral action identified by feminist pastoral theologians. Metaphors and models of the church; word, sacrament and liturgy; community, diversity and justice; and partnership and power—these issues in ecclesiology and church practice are closely related to resisting, empowering, nurturing and liberating. Here the bridge image I used at the beginning of this chapter becomes significant. The Christian community should mediate the faith and love of God to the world, in a way which is both self-critical and critical of oppressive social and political structures. This mediation comes about both through critical theological reflection and engagement with the Christian tradition and through the pastoral action of the community, which is integrally tied to that critical reflection.

The pastoral action of the community involves resisting, empowering, nurturing and liberating. In such activity God is imaged. Resistance to all that damages and brings shame and death mirrors the work of Jesus Christ—his work in the healing of the sick, in the acceptance of the rejected, in the condemnation of cruelty, greed and hypocrisy, and in his courageous facing out of the 'powers that be' even though it cost him his life. Empowerment of all who are silenced and who are weak and despised in the world mirrors the work of the Holy Spirit of God, in giving voice to those who cannot find words and to those whom the world considers foolish, and in giving strength to the weak to act and speak with courage and joy. Nurture mirrors the work of the loving Father and Mother God, who tends and cares for all humanity with infinite love and patience. Liberation mirrors the work of the triune God who sees the suffering and pain of human beings and gives to the uttermost to bring freedom and flourishing.

I would not want, of course, to 'divide up' the work of God; such a way of expressing things is to illustrate the rootedness of pastoral action in the whole nature of God, of the divine. The aspirations of feminist pastoral theologians for the church are not merely pragmatic, and certainly not merely a spillover from the agenda of the world at large; they are rooted in a vision of God. The practical aspects of feminist pastoral care cannot be separated from the vision of the church, which in turn cannot be separated from the vision of God. So our models of the church, our liturgy, our commitment to justice and our exercise of power speak of the kind of God we believe in, and they also radically affect our possibilities for resistance, empowerment, nurture and liberation.

A Vision for the Christian Community—the Pivot

To say that something is pivotal is to say that it is supremely important because it on this that other things turn and depend. The Christian community is thus pivotal as the possibility of the realization of the work of God in the world. It is, however, abundantly clear that particular instances of Christian community, and also those larger communities consisting of various denominations and ecclesial traditions, fall short of reflecting the image of any sort of God in whom it would be decent to believe. The image of God is seriously distorted in the church, not least by violence:

Vision for change and renewal is therefore of the utmost importance:

> Every human being has the innate capacity to dream, and dreaming is a human right which must be respected. Life without dreams is not only humdrum and tedious, but one is also prone to feelings of resignation which act like a powerful virus for which there is no antidote, gradually eroding all desire to live, and leading eventually to nihilism (Tamez 2001: 57).

The 'midrash' we wrote was a kind of dream—a statement that things don't have to be as they are. Feminist theologians writing about the church frequently write about their dreams. Tamez, a Latin American feminist theologian, fills out her dream for the church in terms of joy, quality of life for all, acknowledgment of the work of women, God as guarantor of the new creation, and an ecclesial community free of violence:

> [D]reaming is the eschatological dimension of *ecclesia*. It is entrusted to the pilgrim people to keep the dream alive. Living out of the dream, empowered by God's dream, means giving shape to God's project on earth. As such, this is the most vital dimension of authentic *ecclesia* (Grey 1997: 107).

For dreams to engender the will to live there must be two elements present. The first is images that nurture hope; the second is some reality, some action, however small, that gives substance to the dream and the hope that is not just an empty dream. So both imagination and commitment to act are called for. Metaphors and models, and word sacrament and liturgy, speak particularly of imagination—in envisaging alternative possibilities and in the use of symbols that nurture healing and hope. I draw this chapter to a conclusion with an image of hope for us to nurture.

'Flourishing' is an image which has been recently advocated (e.g. Jantzen 1995b) as a metaphor for Christian hope and vision. The image is drawn from flowers and blossoming. It has strong biblical roots, for example in the vision of Isaiah—'The wilderness and the dry land shall be glad, the desert shall rejoice and blossom' (35.1); and the Psalms—'They are like trees planted by streams of water, which yield their fruit in their season, and their leaves do not wither' (1.3); and in the words of Jesus—'Let anyone who is thirsty come to me, and let the one who believes in me drink. As the scripture has said, "Out of the believer's heart shall flow rivers of living water"' (Jn 7.37-38). Flourishing speaks of growth and thriving, of beauty and nourishment. It is not an individualistic concept—one flourishes as part of a community which is flourishing, and people's flourishing is related to the flourishing of the natural world around them. A community flourishes when it is rooted and grounded in that which gives life—in the presence of God and in the practice of justice and love. Flourishing is a holistic concept; it is difficult with this image to split off the bodily from the spiritual or the mental. Flourishing also implies a cyclical process of natural growth, blossoming, death and rebirth. So often church communities and organizations reach the stage of the beautiful flower or the tasty fruit and then try to hold on to it for ever, not allowing the natural process to move on, and thus becoming a counter sign to their original healthful life. Ecofeminist theologians point to the importance of acknowledging and embracing the natural cycle in contrast to harbouring an obsessive interest in our own survival and importance. Likewise the flourishing community made in the image of God is willing to fall to the ground and die like the seed which will bear new fruit (Jn 12.24).

Flourishing acts as a counter image to violation and violence.

> Then the angel showed me the river of the water of life, bright as crystal, flowing from the throne of God and of the Lamb through the middle of the street of the city. On either side of the river is the tree of life with its twelve kinds of fruit, producing its fruit for each month; and the leaves of the tree are for the healing of the nations (Rev. 22.1-2).

This picture follows the vision of God wiping away every tear, and of the end of death, mourning, crying and pain. The tension between the often destructive reality and the vision of flourishing fuels feminist theology and feminist pastoral action. Such destructiveness and such vision are both found in our Christian communities. For feminist Christian pastoral theologians there is no escape from this tension, for the church is the context of so much of our pastoral practice, and on the question of the church turns and depends the possibility of the love of God made manifest in human community.

Chapter Seven

Women and Pastoral Care

The Cambridge Theological Federation uses one of the local churches for its fortnightly worship together. The inside of this church was completely reordered some years ago. It offers an open and accessible space for the congregation and a large raised area for those involved in leading the service. A close woman friend of mine, a wheelchair user and at the time a student in the Federation preparing for the Anglican priesthood, surveyed the steps leading up to the area for the worship leaders and said ruefully, 'They designed this church thoughtfully for disabled members of the *congregation*, but it doesn't seem to have occurred to them that we might actually be the ones *ministering!*' This incident illustrates poignantly the way in which people are so often divided into those who give pastoral care and those who receive it. The fact that my friend is a priest who uses a wheelchair brings home the sense in which pastoral giving and pastoral need may be located in the same person. What she illustrates vividly is a truth which is applicable to everyone in the Christian community. I propose to examine issues for women as *givers* of pastoral care and as *recipients* of pastoral care in turn in this final chapter—women as carers and as cared for. I hope it will be clear as the exploration proceeds that giving shapes receiving and receiving shapes giving, and that feminist pastoral care is predicated on an assumption of the value of mutuality.

The focus of this book has been feminist pastoral *theology* not feminist pastoral *care*. However, the examination of feminist pastoral theology has been in constant reference to issues of pastoral care, and the questions arising from pastoral care and pastoral needs have structured the theological exploration. For detailed exploration of particular aspects of feminist pastoral care the reader is referred to the fast-growing literature on the subject, a selection of which has been mentioned throughout this book and may be found in the bibliography.[1] In my normal teaching context I expect that participants will

---

1.   See especially Ackermann and Bons-Storm 1998; Bons-Storm 1996; Glaz and

contribute their own experience and engage this with the theoretical feminist perspectives which I offer. That is what I hope the readers of this book will do. In order to earth such analysis of experience, and to *un*earth some of the key issues for feminist pastoral theology in the context of specific care experiences, I will in this chapter seek to analyse from the perspective of gender my own experience as a giver and a receiver of pastoral care. In relation to women as *carers* I shall highlight the questions of appropriate vulnerability, of professionalism and of 'emotional labour'. In relation to women as *cared for* I shall highlight the questions of role and status in church and society, of the actual pastoral needs of women and of pastoral relationships.

A recurring theme of this book has been violence. The concrete reality of violence against women has given the subject matter its urgency; violence has also been the interpretative lens for an analysis of patriarchy and of theology. Feminist pastoral care is sometimes concerned with actual violence against women. At other times it is concerned with issues which are not in any way overtly violent. But the analysis I have made suggests that even where there is not overt violence it is fruitful to examine the effects of the underlying implicit violence of patriarchy.

So it is important to say what this chapter *does* seek to do, and also what it *does not* seek to do. It does seek to examine practices of pastoral care, from the perspective of a feminist analysis of a specific context. I have told this story this way for three reasons. First, it is my story. As a feminist pastoral theologian I consider it important to be prepared to reflect on and theorize my own story as a gendered person. Second, it is an invitation to the reader to engage in the same process, to theorize her or his own story and reflect on its implications. Third, it is vital to note that there are underlying patterns of the operation of patriarchy in church and society which can be identified in all stories, those which unfold in comparatively comfortable and outwardly benign circumstances as well as those which are characterized by extreme violence and pain. What this chapter does not claim to do is to explore in detail circumstances characterized by extreme pain and violence. They have not been part of my story. I looked at such issues in Chapter 2 as a starting point for my analysis, and the reader is referred to literature mentioned there for exploration of those stories which exemplify the extreme and overt violence suffered by many women.[2] Where

Moessner 1991; Gorsuch 2001; Graham 1990; Graham and Halsey 1993; Moessner 1996; Neuger 1996, 2001.

2.   See, for example, Adams and Fortune 1995; Brownmiller 1975; Fortune 1983; Glaz and Moessner 1991: chs. 5–7; Lockley 1999; Mananzan *et al.* 1996; Procter-Smith 1995a; Rutter 1989.

possible, however, in this chapter, I shall make connections with other kinds of stories and experiences than my own.

Women as Carers

My significant roles of pastoral caring began at the age of 21 when I married a Church of England Vicar, who was at the time beginning a new role as a University Chaplain. Although the theory had been that this was to be a shared ministry, I soon learned the hard way what a difference a clerical collar, a paid post and seniority of age would make. Nevertheless, within a few years, both my new status as a Reader in the local church, and also motherhood, gave both the feeling and the reality of actually being engaged in pastoral care and work. At the age of 37 I took up my first salaried post, as a tutor and lecturer in an Anglican theological college training women and men for ordained ministry in the church—a job which brought with it considerable delicate pastoral work both official and unofficial. That work led into my current post as Director of Postgraduate Studies in Pastoral Theology for a Federation of theological teaching institutions. My pastoral involvement is now focused specifically around issues for students of academic guidance, returning to study, relating study to pastoral work, and the personal and corporate crises that arise in the life of any academic community and its members. I am qualified as an academic theologian and as a teacher; I have never been formally trained in pastoral care or counselling.

I have three daughters. I have also been married, divorced, remarried, lived in a step-family and am now separated. Although the context and specifics of my pastoral care for family is quite different from the pastoral care I have exercised in the church or in college, I regard all these aspects of my life and work in caring as of a piece. I cannot split up either the *issues* raised in pastoral care for family, congregation and students, or the *person I am* in relation to each of these. In spite of differences and tensions they are all part of an integrated whole. I propose to identify three issues that arise in my experience as a pastoral carer, and explore these in the light of some theoretical perspectives and in the light of questions posed by feminist analysis. These are vulnerability, professionalism and emotion in its relation to care. All of these issues are related to love and to loving, which I consider to be the heart of Christian pastoral theology and pastoral action (Bennett Moore 1998a). They are all deeply intertwined and will continually overlap in my treatment. The theoretical perspectives underlying my analysis can be found in Hochschild 1983; Campbell 1985; Ross 1988; Herrick and Mann 1998.

Vulnerability

Vulnerability may indicate woundedness from the past, or it may indicate a willingness and openness to be wounded in the present or the future. In theology the idea of the 'wounded healer' has been a widely discussed image of immense fruitfulness, especially since the publication of the work of Henri Nowen on this topic (Campbell 1981; Herrick and Mann 1998; Nouwen 1990 [1972]). This picture of what it is to be a human being in the image of God (Christ) complements a parallel movement in theology to assert the 'vulnerability' of God in face of excessive concentration on God's 'impassibility'— God's being beyond the changes and imperfections of suffering (Moltmann 1974; Vanstone 1977). The vision of woundedness as the imitation of Christ and as the way to mediate God's presence and love in the world may be rooted in the theological idea of incarnation. As Jesus Christ lays aside his power and glory to become a human being, even a vulnerable baby, so Christian discipleship involves immersion in and acceptance of the messiness and suffering of human life. And this 'laying aside' involves a self-emptying' or laying aside of self. The crucifixion is a powerful symbol of vulnerability, in which woundedness brings life and healing. In a rather different way, the contemporary emphasis on the mutuality and love between the 'persons' of the Trinity presents an image of openness and hence vulnerability. In these images can be seen the power of the vision of God to inspire human behaviour. There is, however, a danger of doing the opposite, of imaging God in the light of human behaviour and values. These values and practices may be problematic, but they become harder to question when adorned with the halo of godlikeness. This will be seen to be a danger for women in respect of woundedness and vulnerability.

Vulnerability, both in the sense of having been wounded in the past and in the sense of that commitment and love which lay us open to hurt, may be helpful and fruitful in pastoral relationships. The fact that I have experienced the death of my baby son, and also that I have twice known the rejection and sense of failure that divorce and marriage breakdown brings, allows me levels of empathy and wisdom in pastoral care which I would not otherwise have. This is not a case of 'I know what it feels like' but of a whole change of personality, understanding and even status, which such experiences bring.[3] There are, however, serious limitations to this fruitfulness of vulnerability. For a start, it can be a short move from saying that our wounds may have healing

---

3.   There are circumstances under which explicit airing of the facts or feelings of my own situation would be counterproductive as a burden or a distraction to someone else looking to me for help.

capacities to saying that it is God's will that we are suffering, thus glorifying what should be lamented or resisted. Secondly, there are thousands of women in the world who lose not one child but all their children to starvation, preventable disease or the soldier's bayonet. It would be utterly obscene to speak of this kind of vulnerability in any terms other than determination to put an end to it.

Feminist theologians have generally welcomed an image of God and a way of human caring that invites us to see God, and to join God, identifying with the world in suffering and open to the woundedness which comes from engaged love. Janet Morley's prayers, for example, demonstrate a finely tuned understanding of the symbiotic relationship that is possible between weakness and strength:

> God of the dispossessed,
> defender of the helpless
> you grieve with all the women who weep
> because their children are no more:
> may we also refuse to be comforted
> until the violence of the strong
> has been confounded,
> and the broken victims have been set free… (Morley 1992: 29).

But we must be cautious lest a vision of the vulnerable God reinforce inappropriate vulnerability in women. Maggie Ross illustrates the point:

> The cry of dereliction from the Cross can be likened to our experience of sitting in the dark… It is also, to name a contemporary issue, the experience of being woman, of being woman who in this society has been raped intellectually, psychologically, and spiritually, not to mention physically… [S]he must sit there, damaged and wounded, without hope that her integrity is or can be otherwise (Ross 1988: xix).

When it comes to valuing vulnerability we must take account of the fact that women are differently placed from men, both socially and in the church. Psychologically, materially and spiritually women have been exploited and violated in personal and structural ways, which indicates extreme caution in advocating the language of woundedness for women. Self-sacrifice and denial of self have been imposed as religious ideals on women whose problem is too much self-denial (Bennett Moore 1998a; Gill-Austern 1996; Saiving 1995 [1960]). Women are told to return to damaging marriages as an act of 'taking up their cross daily'. I was advised this myself by a senior churchman. Personally I was *not* being physically abused, but my 'advisor' did not know this, and I am afraid to say many women are thus sent back, in some cases to be beaten and raped. It was only my knowledge and status as a theological teacher and a pastoral carer that enabled me to reply that the theology of the cross in the gospels is far richer and more nuanced than he was implying.

This highlights an important point concerning the extra inappropriate vulnerability experienced by women as a result of a combination of socialization to 'master anger and aggression in the service of "being nice"' (Hochschild 1983: 163) and of a low 'status shield'. 'The lower one's status the more one's feelings are not noticed or treated as inconsequential' (p. 172). While it is important for Christians to understand the kind of 'weakness' in which 'God's strength is made perfect' (2 Cor. 12.9), the kind of weakness which is induced by socialization into low self-esteem and inability to tell one's story, or induced by low esteem accorded by others, is not a kind of weakness which is either godly or fruitful. It is the result of other people's misuse of power.

Professionalism

The pastoral theologian Alastair Campbell (Campbell 1984; 1985) has raised the question of whether Christian pastoral care is currently in captivity to a model of professional expertise. There is a tension between some of the common characteristics of professionalism in care—training, expertise, boundary-keeping and detachment, remuneration, rules and regulations, efficiency, one-sidedness of care—and a Christian vision of love. There is some tension in the notion of efficient loving. As a former colleague of mine wrote in relation to the training of pastors and priests:

> If it is thought that skills can dispense with the need for grace, then they are a counter-sign. Efficient loving is what we are after. And that sounds absurd because what is there about the passion that is efficient? Or about loving (which allows so much hatred to be drawn out of people)? (Westcott House, ACCM 22 submission 1991).

Campbell identifies the following elements as features of the captivity of pastoral care to professional expertise—'lack of mutuality; maldistribution of influence and power; intellectualism; neglect of the communal dimension; and resistance to radical change' (1985: 40). It is immediately apparent that this list coincides substantially with some key concerns of feminist pastoral theologians.

Both the position of 'Vicar's wife' and of college tutor have raised acutely for me issues of professionalism in pastoral care. Some aspects of professionalism (Herrick and Mann 1998: 105) are for me unproblematic. For example, I would regard proper responsibility and accountability to a wider community as features of good pastoral action, preventing improper abuse of authority and status towards the person cared for, such as that identified by Peter Rutter in his discussion of 'when men in power—therapists, doctors, clergy, teachers and others—betray women's trust' (Rutter 1989).

However, those features of professionalism which isolate the 'carer' from her community by putting her in a special and non-reciprocal position cause more difficulties. Women who are in a recognized pastoral role have to deal with questions of 'maldistribution of influence and power' as well as men. Because of patriarchal social and church structures, the issues of power have different contours for women than they do for men, but gender is not the *only* difference which produces power imbalances. Differences of social status, class and education often divide those who are pastoral professionals and those who are cared for. In an ecclesial context the professionals also often have 'power within the system'.[4] Under these circumstances mutuality is hard to achieve, individualism rather than a communal approach to pastoral care is easier, and intellectualism and resistance to radical change result from the social, economic and educational location of the professional carer.

In both parish and college context I have been implicated myself in these processes whereby commitment to mutuality and communal ways of working are eroded, more or less subtly. The particular shape these issues take varies enormously according to context. It is, however, possible to take a view which maximizes the benefits of detachment and protection, or a view which maximizes the benefits of mutual care, trust, responsibility and a holistic view of one's own life and self. I use the word 'benefits' in both cases deliberately. In my own case I have found that a style of pastoral care which maximizes mutuality and integration, seeking to protect the boundaries of self and others while not mistaking fences for genuinely helpful boundaries, has been both personally fulfilling and, I believe, creative for others. If I have deliberately taken risks in making myself vulnerable it has sometimes hurt but I have not regretted it. I do not, however, consider it permissible deliberately to take risks which make *others* vulnerable.

The fluid boundaries between domestic and professional roles experienced by women may be experienced positively or negatively, and for most of us are experienced as ambiguous. Apart from the literal impact on professional work of the care of children and of the 'double shift' of household management which is experienced by women, there is the spillover of the roles and qualities of 'the supportive mother and…the sexually desirable mate' (Hochschild 1983: 181-82). Referring to her research on American flight attendants whose work involves a substantial caring element Hochschild writes:

---

4.   The realities of power imbalance may be complex and not altogether one-sided. See Billman 1996: 16-17.

> [F]emale flight attendants mingle with people who expect them to *enact* two
> leading roles of Womanhood: the loving wife and mother (serving food, tending
> the needs of others) and the glamorous 'career woman' (dressed to be seen, in
> contact with strange men, professional and controlled in manner, and literally
> very far from home). They do the job by symbolizing the transfer of homespun
> femininity into the impersonal marketplace, announcing in effect, 'I work in the
> public eye, but I'm still a woman at heart' (1983: 175).

These fluid boundaries reinforce the tendency to cast women as 'naturally pastoral' and to take advantage of this in professional contexts. For example, women academic tutors report a vicious circle in which the expectation of them beyond the expectation put on their male colleagues to offer pastoral support to students uses up so much time that while the expectations grow the time available diminishes. So when other students find them unavailable, they report this in evaluation forms, and thus the women are penalized for being unavailable to students (Marchbank and Letherby 2002).

Fluidity of boundaries between home and work, between the whole of what one is and what one does, has its benefits in terms of the kind of holistic and integrated approach to pastoral work which many women (and men) would desire. However, since the particular way this works out for women is predicated on a male view and male desire, as Hochschild points out, and also on the material and relational inequalities experienced by women, then much of the benefit to them is at the very least ambivalent. For myself I enjoy and find fruitful the possibilities of integration between home and work, and between myself as a woman, a mother and a professional. However, I have found at times the intrusion of expectations, my own and those of others, derived from 'woman as motherly carer' or 'woman as sexualized enhancer of male self-esteem' both distressing and destructive. The root of the problem lies within the patriarchal character of society.

In addition to raising issues of status and of working practices the concept of 'the professional' implies pay for work done. Women in the church are very often *not* paid for work for which men would be paid. 'Self-stipendiary' clergy in the Church of England are a case in point. An example from a woman who attended the Feminist Perspectives course illustrates this.

> Pam, an Anglican priest, has been working for 4 years unpaid, for part of that time
> looking after a church on her own, because the church would not ordain her to a
> paid post. This was, they said, because she was not deployable to *other* parts of the
> country since her husband could not move his job. Of the people who were
> ordained with her, she found that the 12 women were all working for no pay,
> many several days a week while, of the 12 men, 11 were paid by the church and
> the other had a full time secular job (Bennett Moore 2002b forthcoming).

While this situation may free women from the difficulty of being 'paid to care' (Campbell 1985) or muddling priesthood with having a career (Ross 1988) the fact is that pay is an element of being a professional which brings status as well as material help. Until *all* pastors and priests eschew that status and material help it is scarcely appropriate that it is held up as a vision for women.

Furthermore, women all over the world are 'pillars of the church' as the WCC *Living Letters* documents, often carrying the bulk of the churches' work (WCC 1997: 17). These pillars of the church are not normally its 'professionals', and lack the support provided for professionals. An instructive instance is the wives of clergy,[5] who are in a particularly vulnerable situation in this respect. Lesley Orr MacDonald's work in the 'Out of the Shadows'[6] project has brought to public attention the incidence of abuse in clergy families. One aspect of such situations is the way in which a woman, who may have devoted her life to the church but is not one of its professionals, can be trapped into staying in an abusive relationship because she has no job, no independent means and no house if she leaves.

It is clear therefore that the association of pastoral care with professional expertise has a variety of features which are profoundly ambiguous from a feminist perspective. A critical feminist pastoral theology must attend to the situation of the carer as well as to the dynamics of care—indeed the two are inextricably entwined. The issue of professionalism highlights in particular the social situation and the economic situation of the carer.

Emotional Work
The tension identified above concerning the fluid boundaries between domestic and professional roles cannot be resolved without attention to the question of the 'self' and how the self is identified within caring work. Here again Hochschild's work is full of insight. She makes use of the notion of 'emotional labour' to describe, in conscious alignment with Marx's exploration of alienated physical labour, the process by which emotional 'work' is bought. Her example is the kindness, caring and smiling helpfulness of the flight attendant, who takes abuse and does not get riled, which is typical of the way people may be required to 'manage' their emotions to produce them on behalf of their employer. It is not difficult to see the parallels with pastoral work. The pressure towards sincerity in what is expected of flight attendants is substantial; it

---

5.   In some denominations in parts of the world a woman is only permitted to engage in certain kinds of pastoral work if she is married to a clergyman.

6.   See further Chapter 1 above.

is even greater in the case of those committed to Christian pastoral work, for whom the goal of genuine love and generous self-giving in the service of God do not allow the kind of distancing of self from role which flight attendants may be allowed.

Hochschild analyses how even in the case of flight attendants there is a real tension between overidentification with role which produces burnout, and distancing from role which produces alienation and a feeling of being 'phoney' (1983: 188). She shows clearly how the problems of this self–role tension are gendered, as women more straightforwardly identify with a role that demands passivity in the face of aggression and blows to self-esteem, and continuous caring for others at the expense of self.

There is a further gendered aspect to this. Self-assertion may be an insufficient answer. For women the retention of a core inner self, separate from the wider needs of group and community, may not be what they desire. It is difficult to disentangle whether and where women's desire to find self *in relating* is a false altruistic self imposed by patriarchal deformation, and where this relational self is a healthy expression of what women truly desire. As a result, when women experience fulfilment in meeting the needs of others in altruistic mode it may indicate either a true living out of their selfhood or a distorted self-understanding. However, such a situation is at the very least open to abuse since 'the altruist is more susceptible to being used—not because her sense of self is weaker but because her "true self" is bonded more securely to the group and its welfare' (Hochschild 1983: 196). Such an analysis goes beyond the simple dichotomy of self-fulfilment versus self-denial, and indicates the importance of a gendered analysis of both professional emotional 'labour' and the emotional work done within families. As women increasingly are identified as pastoral agents—as they are included in professional roles and as 'emotional work' within family and community is recognized and reflected upon—then the question of how women and their work as pastoral carers are affected by the structural and psychological effects of patriarchy must continually be posed.

Women as Cared For

Reflection from a gendered perspective on my own history of being cared for pastorally yields three particular areas of interest—role and status in church and society, pastoral needs, and pastoral relationships. I shall treat each of these in turn, drawing from my own experience and raising questions from this for the pastoral care of women.

Role and Status

My journey of being cared for in specifically Christian contexts began when I was 15 and joined the local Evangelical Anglican church. My parents were not at the time churchgoers, and it was from my point of view coincidental that I joined this particular church, which happened to be at the top of my street. There was a thriving youth group which I joined and it was from the leadership of this group that I received pastoral care. It was good pastoral care in that it involved both concern for my whole life not just my church life, and it also involved an expectation that as I grew in faith and understanding I would play my part in the pastoral care of others. In spite of the fact that at the time women were not ordained in the Church of England, the church youth culture in which I was nurtured clearly recognized that both women and men had gifts of ministry. The emphasis at that time (1960s) among Anglican Evangelicals in Britain was that women should not hold positions of *leadership*, except in so far as these were held under the authority of a man, or perhaps in partnership with a man. This assumption was rooted, or so it came over to me, in a combination of scriptural teaching and the 'common sense' attitude that women were normally not as suited as men to leadership, and that anyway if a woman was in charge it would make the boys think the set-up was sissy. Unfortunately therefore my first and formative context of pastoral care reinforced an attitude I had already picked up from my father, that girls and women might indeed be very able but that in the end they were less suited to being the front runners in 'the real world'. Men, in this scenario, are the gateway to the real and public world, and in Peter Rutter's words:

> it is a damaging judgement that communicates to [women] that what they have to offer to the world outside the home is less valuable than what men have to offer, and that the particularly feminine values they carry are a liability in the workplace, the political arena, and in public life.
>
> As a result women feel that their lives are closed in, restricted, and impaired (Rutter 1989: 83-84).

Rutter in *Sex in the Forbidden Zone* is specifically interested in how this situation leads to the sexual abuse of women by men who hold the keys to the outside world for them. The damage to women's psychological health, self-confidence and possibilities in life is, however, widespread even when such damage does not lead to sexual abuse.

In my own case it is no coincidence that I ended up marrying the curate who led this youth group and was ten years my senior. By marrying my primary pastoral carer I allowed the dynamics of both care and leadership from the public church zone to become merged with the dynamics of my marriage relationship—a merging which at the time seemed creative, but which later proved problematic.

Being a 'vicar's wife' structured my self-perception and my public role and status for 17 years. My image was borrowed from another person; I was defined in relation to that other person's role and status. It was when I left my husband—and the vicarage—and subsequently got divorced that the pastoral care issues for myself became very much gendered. As a clergy wife I had never done more than a little part-time work. I had kept house, looked after the children, offered hospitality and been involved in church work. The house was not ours and I had no personal pension. My situation was therefore that I had to move out of the vicarage and that I had no savings or pension. These things were directly related to my role and position. No help was forthcoming from the official church. What is more, the kind of pastoral support I could receive from the church community I had been part of was curtailed drastically by the official injunction that we should not talk about our problems in the congregation, but that I should just go and let others explain when I had gone. Men took all the decisions here and told the story.

Underlying this narrative concerning roles are the dominant sociocultural, psychological and theological narratives which Bons-Storm (1996) identifies as defining women's roles and as silencing women's stories and hindering their ability to become subjects in their own right. Through pastoral care I entered a prescribed narrative and role as an Evangelical Christian woman and clergy wife. Even in my assertion of my own 'rebellion' against this, my story and the pastoral care I received were taken over by another prescribed role and narrative—of women who leave their clergy husbands.

I do, however, support Bons-Storm's suggestion that both men and women, if they attend courageously to the problems raised for women by the dominant roles and narratives, may offer pastoral care which subverts them. In subsequent pastoral care I have experienced this. Sometimes it has been given spontaneously; sometimes I have had painfully to challenge expectations and behaviour, and have been met with understanding and repentance.

Pastoral Needs

Looking back over my own life story I would identify the following areas of significant pastoral needs, all of which have gender-related dimensions— motherhood and the bringing up of three daughters, financial and work issues, understanding my sexuality and sexual relationships, and the need for confidence.

Motherhood. Being a mother has constructed the person I am, the life I live and the relationships I have. From my experience I see a whole range of areas of pastoral concern. There are material questions about the practical help which mothers, and particularly those who are living alone with children, need. In many cultures, including a powerful strand in current British political rhetoric, there is stigma attached to being divorced or a single mother which has economic implications.[7] There are political questions about maternity pay and conditions, nursery and childcare provision, health and education for children. There are political and religious questions about family planning and contraception. There are questions about the institution of marriage and how it is related to motherhood which are both political and ethical questions. There are questions about how motherhood is construed and how pressures are put on mothers in the service of political or theological ideology. For instance, it is said that if women stay at home they don't take men's jobs, if women bond with their children it enhances the children's psychological health, and women are responsible for creating the supportive home environment in which men and children flourish. There are questions about identity and self and the way mothers allow their own needs to be submerged in their children's needs. There are questions about the responsible bringing up of children in contemporary society. All these are necessary areas for pastoral reflection and action.[8]

Financial and Work Matters. Women often have pastoral needs related to financial and work matters. I have mentioned that I started a career late and with it the earning of independent means and a personal pension. That I did so is directly connected to expectations on me as a woman, to motherhood and also to priorities and choices I have made from my perspective as a woman brought up in a particular Christian environment. Human flourishing is affected by the provision of material needs and also by opportunities to be creative in work, and the possibility of taking responsibility for oneself and one's family. Pastoral care of women must attend to such issues in a way that addresses not only individual needs but the social context in which they arise.

Expectations on women, what work they will do and what financial security they will have, of course vary in different cultural contexts. When I have complained to my Feminist Perspectives class of the 'double shift' expected of many Western women, I have more than once been informed by men participating in

7. There is also in many cultures stigma attached to being single or to being childless. This too may have economic implications.

8. See further Miller-McLemore 1994.

the class from other parts of the world that in some contexts women are expected not only to look after the children, but to work in the fields, carry the water and take the whole responsibility for the household's well-being. Mary Grey's heartbreaking account of the women in Rajasthan who carry immense burdens of work and care for the family, but are (ill)treated as worthless parasites, widens the perspective still further (Grey 2000b). In the situations of women across the world there is an underlying continuity and there are radical differences. Feminist pastoral theology must take account of both.

Sexual Relationships and the Need for Confidence. In respect of sexual relationships I really wish the church could say more to most of us than 'if I were you I wouldn't start from there!' Of course that is a generalization, but I have found as a woman who has experienced two marriage break-ups that it is difficult to find explorations of Christian moral understanding that touch my experience. What is more, in my daughters I see a new generation of young people who seek to act responsibly in their sexual relationships, but who find little said from a Christian perspective which engages with the world in which they live.[9]

But it is not only a matter of sexual *behaviour*; it is a matter of understanding ourselves as sexual beings. For me the issue of sexuality and God is so important because it has to do with the 'godlikeness' of such an essential part of ourselves. The implications of the work of feminists such as Catherine Mac-Kinnon concerning the inevitable violence of heterosexism raise questions for me as a heterosexual woman about the connections between spirituality and sexuality (see Adams 1995). It was certainly my experience that the primary image of a 'father-figure' God who protected but who also demanded obedience shaped my sexual relationships with men, and also shaped my expectations of pastoral care from men. As my understanding of God has changed and developed maturity so has my understanding of my relationships with men and of the kind of pastoral care I desire and expect.

This is directly related to the need for confidence I identified earlier. I have fought for self-confidence as a woman in the face of the kind of role, status and character for women projected by my father and my early Christian teaching, which made men the gateway to the real world. This struggle is further complicated by the view of men as protectors and decision-makers implicit in my theological and psychological understanding of God, sex and

9. Adrian Thatcher's writing on the subject of marriage and sexual relationships is a serious attempt to engage with the contemporary context in an way that is both imaginative and faithful to the Christian tradition (Thatcher 1999), but I do not find in his work a deep engagement with the situations in which my family finds itself.

pastoral care. In my pastoral work I have been astonished to discover many women with problems of self-confidence greatly in excess of my own. A major project in the pastoral care of women is the restoration of self-confidence and a genuine sense of themselves as responsible subjects of their own lives (Bons-Storm 1996: 146).[10]

Pastoral Relationships
My pastoral relationships with men have had significantly different features from my pastoral relationships with women. An examination of the differences illuminates some important issues in the pastoral care of women. I can identify at least three significant aspects of my relationships with men who have offered pastoral care to me. The first is that for many years the dual role which men played as protectors and as gateways to the real world affected my relationships with male pastoral carers in an adverse way. I can identify this projection onto my curate/husband, doctors, other clergy, professors and academic supervisors. It made me dependent and gullible; it also introduced a dynamic of sexual and of spiritual need which was transferred from the corresponding unsatisfactory nature of my view of sexual relationships and of God. In this context I was dependent on there not being an answering projection of need or dependency from male carers. In most cases there was not; sometimes there was. Where there was I had to work extra hard to cope not only with my original problems, but also the additional ones which my relationships with male pastoral carers brought about. Coming to a resolution of this unsatisfactory pattern of relating is not just a matter of curing the dependent or hysterical woman; it is a matter of understanding the complex patterns of behaviour and psychology set up in men and women by the patriarchal patterns of society.[11]

My relationships with the women who have offered me pastoral care have always been on a much more equal and mutual basis. These have often grown out of communal contexts. For example, during the period my children were young I was a founder member of a flourishing group of young mums and children in the local church, of which my husband was the vicar. Meeting at

10. I have viewed the issue of pastoral needs, sexuality and self-confidence through the lens of my heterosexual experience. Lesbian women have a different viewpoint, and some of their experiences of being silenced, devalued and excluded are different from those of heterosexual women. For direct accounts of these see Alison Webster's *Found Wanting* (1995).

11. For more detailed treatment of questions of psychology and counselling see Gorsuch (2001), Neuger (2001).

least twice a week for formal activities and then continually in one another's homes, we supported each other through the birth and death of babies, through marital crises, through the finding and the loss of faith, through illness and through joy. We prayed together, we sang together, we ate fish and chips together, we complained together and we pushed our children in the park together. There was not a shred of feminist consciousness among us, but we had plenty of woman-power! Within this group particular friends offered different kinds of love, support and advice according to their experience and their characters.

A second example is more recent. Two friends and I, some 20 years older and wiser than my group of mums, sit in silent prayer together, talk, discuss theology, go to concerts and eat together. We are each individually friends and we are friends as a group. We have held each other through crises. As we have talked through issues we have brought to them our understanding of patriarchy and its effects.

The desire for mutuality in pastoral relationships is most easily satisfied in such contexts. I have learned about this kind of relating from my relationships with women. At the end of her chapter on 'Gender Imagery for God/ess' in *Womanguides* (1985a: 8) Rosemary Radford Ruether suggests an exercise which involves imagining and drawing 'a symbol for yourself and for God/ess', first when conceived in male terms, and second when conceived in female terms. My first 'male' picture is of the sun shining strongly down, with embracing warmth and protecting strength on me, a lone figure. My second 'female' picture is of a whole group of figures in a circle, holding hands and talking with one of the figures who somehow stands out but is still very much part of the group. My pictures of 'God' did not surprise me; what interested me was the change in the significance of other people.

Feminist Pastoral Theology

As would be expected, women are found to be particularly susceptible to the distortions of human relating produced by the patriarchal nature of society, both in their roles as pastoral carers and as those who are cared for. The call to vulnerability, to openness and to the altruistic offering of emotional work may bring out characteristics and patterns of working which are congenial to women, but may also leave women precisely more 'vulnerable' to being used and abused in inappropriate ways. As pastoral care work is increasingly professionalized women may find also themselves particularly subject to 'maldistribution of power' and pay. The violent inequalities of patriarchy are clearly manifest in the roles and status of women, in their life and career patterns, in their access, or lack of it, to the public world of power, in their sexual lives and in the pastoral care they receive. The potential for violence, covert and overt, is increased by the overlapping of social, sexual and pastoral roles and understandings.

The Christian tradition includes a positive valuing of love and equality which may be shown in mutuality and care. Jesus' statement that he came not to be served but to serve has been held up as a model to emulate. But in practice hierarchicalism, the use of 'lesser mortals' including women to do the serving, the concepts of male headship and the greater likeness of the male to God, and sexual definitions of women which demean or which consign to subservient roles, all conspire to undermine the vision of genuine mutual service and love.

Neither an image of God that promotes male dominance over women, nor an image of God that promotes dependency and a negative view of self in women, are helpful within pastoral theology. The image of a God who gives in love, who came to serve, and indeed whose love is vulnerable even unto death, is an ambiguous image for women. It is ambiguous because although it holds up an ideal of mutuality and love, in feeling and action, which reflects the values of feminist pastoral theology, it also holds up an ideal of self-giving and self-denial and suffering which has been used, sometimes violently, to reinforce the subservient state of women. Since any images of God are dependent for their value and meaning on the practices of the community which uses them, that ambiguity can only be resolved by the *actions* of Christian communities. Thus are the 'symbols turned'.

Postscript

In the Introduction I described three principles which would guide the shape of this book: that it is appropriate for feminist pastoral theology to start from life experience and to move to a theorizing of that experience and to a critique of existing theory, that feminist pastoral theology will involve a critique of existing Christian beliefs and doctrines, and finally that the aim of feminist pastoral theology is to renew and to transform belief and practice.

The life experience on which I have drawn has been diverse. It has included my own, my friends', that of the women whom I have taught or for whom I have had pastoral care, and that of which I have read or heard in the media. I called this book an 'active journeying to wholeness'; it has been such a journey for me as much as I hope it has for the reader. The journey is painful as it involves facing difficult issues in our own lives, and also listening with empathy to the stories of lives quite different from our own. Violence and violation are not comfortable things to talk about. There has not been quite such a tidy trajectory through the book—from experience, to theoretical analysis, to renewal of practice—as I perhaps originally envisaged, but that in itself reflects (I hope) as much the unruliness of life, ministry and writing as it does my own disorganization. Experience and interpretation and transformation are not wholly distinguishable categories, and they have regularly, or rather *irregularly*, intruded on one another's space in the writing of this book.

The critique of existing Christian beliefs and doctrines has, I hope, included both deconstruction and reconstruction. When I made the decision to put violence, as concrete reality and as theoretical lens, at the beginning of the book, I did not at the time realize how all pervasive the issue of violence would become in it. For some readers there will have been too much deconstruction, and they will feel I have called 'violence! violence! where there is no violence'. But for others there will have been a too quick or optimistic *re*construction, a too ready acceptance of traditional Christian categories. For myself, I stand in a place which *I* am still convinced is the place of the proclamation of the good news of Jesus Christ, preached by him, lived by him, and embodied in crucifixion and resurrection by him, although the images, words and practices I would use in response to the God of that place might sit uncomfortably with those of many Christian traditions. For some, however, that is not to take seriously enough the very critique I have outlined.

So finally, what of the renewal and transformation of belief and practice? In the Introduction I referred to theological education as a place for the building of healing and transforming communities, and to my situation in the profoundly ambivalent relationship between the academic discipline of pastoral theology and the institutional church. I have always been convinced that teaching is itself a pastoral practice (and teaching pastoral theology is a complex self-reflective pastoral practice). Teaching is a discipline which demands that those who do it are both theoreticians and practitioners. People write books in different ways; the way I have written this book has been as a practitioner of teaching who is also a theorizer. And so there has perhaps been in it more theoretical reflection than in many books of the same genre. For some perhaps there has been too much, but my hope is that the glimpses of transformation and healing which I have been able to offer as a practitioner of theological education have been enough to inspire others to hope and work for 'flashes of alternative possibilities' in their own areas of life and work.

By asking theological questions—about the nature of God, the meaning of Jesus Christ for today, the meaning of sin and salvation, the nature of the church—in the context of pastoral issues, I hope I have made a contribution to the priority for feminist pastoral theology which I identified in the Introduction, 'the dialogue between feminist pastoral theology and traditions of Christian belief and Christian ministry'. By making the issue of violence a central theme of my exploration, both as a disturbing reality and as a lens through which to understand the nature of patriarchy and its effects in Christian traditions, I hope to have demonstrated that the concerns of a specifically *feminist* pastoral theology are both desperately serious and global in their implications.

Bibliography

Ackermann, D.M., and R. Bons-Storm (eds.)
    1998   *Liberating Faith Practices: Feminist Practical Theologies in Context* (Leuven: Peeters).

Adams, C.J.
    1995   'Towards a Feminist Theology of Religion and the State', *TheolSex* 2: 61-83.

Adams, C.J., and M.M. Fortune (eds.)
    1995   *Violence Against Women and Children: A Theological Sourcebook* (New York: Continuum).

Armstrong, K.
    1990   'The Acts of Paul and Thecla', in Loades 1990: 83-90.

Baker-Fletcher, K.
    1993   'Anna Julia Cooper and Soujourner Truth: Two Nineteenth-Century Black Feminist Interpreters of Scripture', in Schüssler Fiorenza 1993b: 41-51.

Bal, M.
    1989   'Introduction', in M. Bal (ed.), *Anti-Covenant: Counter-Reading Women's Lives in the Hebrew Bible* (Sheffield: Sheffield Academic Press): 11-28.

Ballard, P., and P. Couture
    1999   *Globalisation and Difference: Practical Theology in a World Context* (Cardiff: Cardiff Academic Press).

Ballard, P., and J. Pritchard
    1996   *Practical Theology in Action: Christian Thinking in the Service of Church and Society* (London: SPCK).

Barth, K.
    1962   *Theology and Church: Shorter Writings 1920–1928* (London: SCM Press).

Barton, J.
    1992   'Review of REB and NRSV', *JTS* 43: 548-50.

Behr-Sigel, E., and Kallistos Ware
    2000   *The Ordination of Women in the Orthodox Church* (Geneva: WCC).

Belenky, M.F., et al.
    1986   *Women's Ways of Knowing: The Development of Self, Voice, and Mind* (New York: Basic Books).

Benhabib, S.
    1992   *Situating the Self: Gender, Community and Postmodernism in Contemporary Ethics* (Cambridge: Polity Press).

Bennett Humphries, I.
    2000   *Race, Gender and Oppression: A Case Study of Arab Women in Israel* (MA thesis, Centre for Middle Eastern and Islamic Studies, University of Durham).

Bennett Moore, Z.
  1997–98   'On Copyclerks, Transformers and Spider: Teachers and Learners in Adult
            Theological Education', *BJTE* 9.2: 36-44.
  1998a   'Women and the Cost of Loving: Towards Transformative Christian
            Practice', *Contact* 127: 11-16.
  1998b   'A Midrash', *FemTh* 18: 29-40.
  2002a   'Creative Risk-taking: Feminist Pedagogy and Assessment Criteria', in
            Howie and Tauchert (eds.).
  2002b   'Leadership as Vocation', in…(Geneva: WCC, forthcoming).
Berger, T.
  1999   *Women's Ways of Worship: Gender Analysis and Liturgical History* (Collegeville,
            MN: Liturgical Press).
Billman, K.D.
  1996   'Pastoral Care as an Art of Community', in Neuger 1996: 10-38.
Bird, P.A.
  1991   'Sexual Differentiation and Divine Image in the Genesis Creation Texts',
            in Børresen 1991b: 5-28.
Bons-Storm, R.
  1996   *The Incredible Woman: Listening to Women's Silences in Pastoral Care and Coun-
            seling* (Nashville: Abingdon Press).
Børresen, K.E.
  1991a   'God's Image, Man's Image? Patristic Interpretation of Gen. 1.27 and I
            Cor. 2.7', in Børresen 1991b: 187-209.
Børresen, K.E. (ed.)
  1991b   *The Image of God: Gender Models in Judeao-Christian Tradition* (Oslo: Solum
            Forlag).
Brenner, A., and Carol Fontaine (eds.)
  1997   *A Feminist Companion to Reading the Bible: Approaches, Methods and Strategies*
            (FCB, 11; Sheffield: Sheffield Academic Press).
Brock, R.N.
  1988   *Journeys by Heart: A Christology of Erotic Power* (New York: Crossroad).
Brooten, B.
  1985   'Early Christian Women and their Cultural Context', in A.Y. Collins (ed.),
            Feminist Perspectives on Biblical Scholarship (Chico, CA: Scholars Press):
            65-69.
Brownmiller, S.
  1975   *Against Our Will: Men, Women and Rape* (London: Secker & Warburg).
Butler, J.
  1990   *Gender Trouble: Feminism and the Subversion of Identity* (London: Routledge).
Byrne, L.
  1994   *Woman at the Altar* (London: Cassell, Petter, Galpin & Co.).
Cahoy, W.J.
  1995   'One Species or Two? Kierkegaard's Anthropology and the Feminist Cri-
            tique of the Concept of Sin', *Modern Theology* 11: 429-54.
Campbell, A.V.
  1981   *Rediscovering Pastoral Care* (London: Darton, Longman & Todd).
  1984   *Moderated Love: A Theology of Professional Care* (London: SPCK).
  1985   *Paid to Care: The Limits of Professionalism in Pastoral Care* (London: SPCK).

Carlson Brown, J., and R. Parker
    1989   For God so Loved the World?', in J. Carlson Brown and C.R. Bohn (eds.), *Christianity, Patriarchy and Abuse: A Feminist Critique* (New York: Pilgrim Press): 1-30.
Carr, A.
    1988   *Transforming Grace* (San Francisco: Harper & Row).
Carr, W.
    1997   *Handbook of Pastoral Studies* (London: SPCK).
Castelli, E.
    1994   'Romans', in Schüssler Fiorenza 1994: 272-300.
Chopp, R.
    1995   *Saving Work: Feminist Practices in Theological Education* (Louisville, KY: Westminster/John Knox Press).
Chung, S.-J.
    2001   'Women Church in Korea: Voices and Visions', *Ecumenical Review* 53: 72-81.
Clebsch, W.A., and C.R. Jaekle
    1975   *Pastoral Care in Historical Perspective* (New York: Jason Aaronson).
Clinebell, H.
    2000   'Greening Pastoral Care to Reciprocally Heal Persons and the Earth', *Contact* 133: 3-12.
CMS, USPG, Methodist Church
    1999   *The Christ We Share*.
Code, L.
    1987   *Epistemic Responsibility* (Hanover, NH: University Press of New England).
    1991   *What Can She Know? Feminist Theory and the Construction of Knowledge* (Ithaca, NY: Cornell University Press).
Couture, P., and R. Hunter (eds.)
    1995   *Pastoral Care and Social Conflict* (Nashville: Abingdon Press).
Crawford, J.
    2001   'Women and Ecclesiology: Two Ecumenical Streams?', *Ecumenical Review* 53: 14-24.
Daggers, J.
    2001   'Feminist Theology as Christo/alogical Revisioning', *FemTh* 27: 116-28.
Dalarun, J.
    1992   'The Clerical Gaze', in Klapisch-Zuber 1992: 15-42.
Daly, M.
    1986   *Beyond God the Father: Towards a Philosophy of Women's Liberation* (London: Women's Press).
    1988   *Websters' First New Intergalactic Wickedary of the English Language, Conjured by Mary Daly in Cahoots with Jane Caputi* (London: Women's Press).
    1993   *Outercourse: The Bedazzling Voyage* (London: Women's Press).
D'Costa, G.
    2000   *Sexing the Trinity: Gender, Culture and the Divine* (London: SCM Press).
De Marinis, V.
    1993   *Critical Caring: A Feminist Model for Pastoral Psychology* (Louisville, KY: Westminster/John Knox Press).
Dixon, L.
    2000   'Reflections on Pastoral Care from a Womanist Perspective', *Contact* 132: 3-10.

Doehring, C.
　　1999　　'A Method of Feminist Pastoral Theology', in Miller-McLemore and Gill-
　　　　　　Austern 1999: 95-111.
Douglass, J.D.
　　1991　　'The Image of God in Women as Seen by Luther and Calvin', in Børresen
　　　　　　1991: 236-66.
Duby, G., and P.M. Perrot (eds.)
　　1992　　*A History of Women in the West* (Cambridge MA: The Belknap Press of
　　　　　　Harvard University Press).
Dulles, A.
　　1976　　*Models of the Church* (Dublin: Gill & MacMillan).
Dworkin, A.
　　1981　　*Pornography: Men Possessing Women* (London: The Women's Press).
Eco, U.
　　1983　　*The Name of the Rose* (London: Secker & Warburg).
Elford, J.
　　1999　　*The Pastoral Nature of Theology: An Upholding Presence* (London: Cassell,
　　　　　　Petter, Galpin & Co.).
Elwes, T. (ed.)
　　1992　　*Women's Voices* (London: Marshall Pickering).
Exum, J.C.
　　1994　　'Second Thoughts about Secondary Characters: Women in Exodus 1.8–
　　　　　　2.10', in A. Brenner (ed.), *A Feminist Companion to Exodus to Deuteronomy*
　　　　　　(FCB, 6; Sheffield: Sheffield Academic Press): 75-87.
Field-Bibb, J.
　　1991　　*Women Towards Priesthood: Ministerial Politics and Feminist Praxis* (Cambridge:
　　　　　　Cambridge University Press).
Figes, K.
　　1994　　*Because of Her Sex: The Myth of Equality for Women in Britain* (London: Mac-
　　　　　　millan).
FitzGerald, K.K. (ed.)
　　1999　　*Orthodox Women Speak: Discerning the Signs of the Times* (Geneva: WCC).
Fontaine, C.R.
　　1997　　'The Abusive Bible: On the Use of Feminist Method in Pastoral Contexts',
　　　　　　in Brenner and Fontaine 1997: 84-113.
Fortune, M.M.
　　1983　　*Sexual Violence: The Unmentionable Sin—An Ethical and Pastoral Perspective*
　　　　　　(New York: Pilgrim Press).
Friedan, B.
　　1963　　*The Feminine Mystique* (London: Gollancz).
Fulkerson, M.M.
　　1994　　*Changing the Subject* (Philadelphia: Fortress Press).
Gelder, A.
　　1996　　'Complementarity', in Isherwood and MacEwan 1996: 33-34.
Giddens, A.
　　1989　　*Sociology* (Cambridge: Polity Press).
Gill-Austern, B.
　　1996　　'Love Understood as Self-Sacrifice and Denial: What Does it do to
　　　　　　Women?', in Moessner 1996: 304-21.

1999   'Pedagogy Under the Influence of Feminism and Womanism', in Miller-McLemore and Gill-Austern 1999: 149-68.

Gilligan, C.
1993   *In a Different Voice: Pyschological Theory and Women's Development* (Cambridge, MA: Harvard University Press).

Glaz, M., and J.S. Moessner
1991   *Women in Travail and Transition: A New Pastoral Care* (Minneapolis: Augsburg–Fortress).

Gnanadason, A.
2001   'Editorial', *Ecumenical Review* 53: 1-4.

Gorsuch, N.
2001   *Introducing Feminist Pastoral Care and Counseling* (New York: Pilgrim Press).

Gössmann, E.
1993   'History of Biblical Interpretation by European Women', in Schüssler Fiorenza 1993b: 27-40.

Graham, E.L.
1990   'Pastoral Theology, Feminism and the Future', *Contact* 103: 2-9.
1996   *Transforming Practice: Pastoral Theology in an Age of Uncertainty* (London: Mowbray).
1998   'A View from a Room: Feminist Practical Theology from Academy, Kitchen or Sanctuary?', in Ackermann and Bons Storm: 129-52.
1999a   'From "Terrible Silence" to "Transforming Hope": The Impact of Feminist Theory on Practical Theology', *International Journal of Practical Theology* 2: 185-212.
1999b   'Pastoral Theology: Therapy, Mission or Liberation?' *SJT* 52: 430-54.
1999c   'Towards a Practical Theology of Embodiment', in Ballard and Couture 1999: 79-84.
2001   *Representations of the Post/Human: Monsters, Aliens and Others in Popular Culture* (Manchester: Manchester University Press).

Graham, E., and M. Halsey (eds.)
1993   *Life Cycles: Women and Pastoral Care* (London: SPCK).

Grant, J.
1989   *White Woman's Christ and Black Woman's Jesus: Feminist Christology and Womanist Response* (Atlanta: Scholars Press).

Greider, K.J., G.A. Johnson and K.J. Leslie
1999   'Three Decades of Women Writing for Our Lives', in Miller-McLemore and Gill-Austern 1999: 21-50.

Grey, M.
1989   *Redeeming the Dream: Feminism, Redemption and Christian Tradition* (London: SPCK).
        'Feminist Theology: Late Arrival or Changeling in the Academy?', *Louvain Studies* 18: 318-32.
1997   *Beyond the Dark Night: A Way Forward for the Church?* (London: Cassell, Petter, Galpin & Co.)
2000a   *The Outrageous Pursuit of Hope: Prophetic Dreams for the Twenty-First Century* (London: Darton, Longman & Todd).
2000b   'Gender, Justice and Poverty in Rural Rajasthan—Moving Beyond the Silence', *FemTh* 25: 33-45.

2001   *Introducing Feminist Images of God* (IFT, 7; Sheffield: Sheffield Academic
          Press).

Hampson, D.
1990   *Theology and Feminism* (Oxford: Basil Blackwell).

Hampson, D., and R.R. Ruether
1987   'Is There a Place for Feminists in the Christian Church?', *New Blackfriars*
          68: 7-24.

Haraway, D.
1991   *Cyborgs, Simians and Women* (London: Polity Press).

Hayter, M.
1987   *The New Eve in Christ: The Use and Abuse of the Bible in the Debate about
          Women in the Church* (London: SPCK).

Held, V. (ed.)
1995   *Justice and Care: Essential Readings in Feminist Ethics* (Colorado: Westview
          Press).

Herrick, V., and I. Mann
1998   *Jesus Wept: Reflections on Vulnerability in Leadership* (London: Darton, Longman
          & Todd).

Hilkert, M.C.
1995   'Cry Beloved Image: Rethinking the Image of God', in A. O'Hara Graff
          (ed.), *In the Embrace of God: Feminist Approaches to Theological Anthropology*
          (Maryknoll, NY: Orbis Books): 190-205.

Hiltner, S.
1958   *Preface to Pastoral Theology* (Nashville: Abingdon Press).

Hochschild, A.
1983   *The Managed Heart: Commercialization of Human Feeling* (Berkeley: University
          of California Press).

Hogan, L.
1995   *From Women's Experience to Feminist Theology* (Sheffield: Sheffield Academic
          Press).

hooks, b.
1984   *Feminist Theory: From Margin to Center* (Boston: South End Press).
1994   *Teaching to Transgress: Education as the Practice of Freedom* (New York: Rout-
          ledge & Kegan Paul).

Hopkins, J.
1995   *Towards a Feminist Christology* (London: SPCK).

Howie, G. and A. Taubert (eds.)
2002   *Gender, Teaching and Research in Higher Education* (Aldershot: Ashgate).

Humphries, N.
2001   *Are Women-Only Utopias the Most Successful Form of Feminist Utopia?* (Under-
          graduate dissertation, Department of Politics, University of Durham).

Hunt, M.
1992   *Fierce Tenderness: A Feminist Theology of Friendship* (New York: Crossroad).

Ind, J.
1993   *Fat is a Spiritual Issue: My Journey* (London: Mowbray).

Isherwood, L., and E. Stuart
1998   *Introducing Body Theology* (IFT, 2; Sheffield: Sheffield Academic Press).

Isherwood, L., and D. McEwan (eds.)
    1996   *An A–Z of Feminist Theology* (Sheffield: Sheffield Academic Press).

Jantzen, G.
    1995a   *Power, Gender and Christian Mysticism* (Cambridge: Cambridge University Press).
    1995b   'Feminism and Flourishing: Gender and Metaphor in Feminist Theology', *FemTh* 10: 81-101.

Jasper, A.
    1998   *The Shining Garment of the Text: Gendered Readings of John's Prologue* (JSNTSup, 165; GCT, 6; Sheffield: Sheffield Academic Press).

Jeffreys, S.
    1992   '"Pornography" and "Creating the Sexual Future": Extracts from "Anti-climax"', in E. Frazer, J. Hornsby and S. Lovibond (eds.), *Ethics: A Feminist Reader* (Oxford: Basil Blackwell): 459-88.

John Paul II
    1981   *The Original Unity of Man and Woman: Catechesis on the Book of Genesis* (Boston: Daughters of Paul).

Johnson, E.A.
    1997   *She Who Is: The Mystery of God in Feminist Theological Discourse* (New York: Crossroad).

Kingsolver, B.
    1998   *The Poisonwood Bible* (USA: HarperCollins).

Kinukawa, H.
    forthcoming   (Geneva: WCC).

Klapisch-Zuber, C. (ed.)
    1992   *A History of Women in the West*. II. *Silences of the Middle Ages* (Cambridge, MA: The Belknap Press of Harvard University Press).

Kroeger, C.C., M. Evans and E. Storkey (eds.)
    1995   *The Women's Study New Testament: Based on the* NRSV (London: Marshall Pickering).

Kwok, P.-l.
    1997   'Overlapping Communities and Multicultural Hermeneutics', in Brenner and Fontaine 1997: 203-215.
    2000   *Introducing Asian Feminist Theology* (IFT, 4; Sheffield: Sheffield Academic Press).

Lartey, E.Y.
    1997   *In Living Colour: An Intercultural Approach to Pastoral Care and Counselling* (London: Cassell, Petter, Galpin & Co.).

Lerner, G.
    1986   *The Creation of Patriarchy* (Oxford: Oxford University Press).

Lewis, C.S.
    1970   'Priestesses in the Church?', in W. Hooper (ed.), *God in the Dock: Essays on Theology and Ethics* (Grand Rapids: Eerdmans):

Loades, A. (ed.)
    1990   *Feminist Theology: A Reader* (London: SPCK).

Lockley, P.
    1999   *Counselling Women in Violent Relationships* (London: Free Association).

MacKinnon, C.A.
 1984 'Not a Moral Issue', *Yale Law and Policy Review* 2.2.
 1989 *Towards a Feminist Theory of the State* (Cambridge, MA: Harvard University Press).
MacKinnon, M.H., and M. McIntyre (eds.)
 1995 *Readings in Ecology and Feminist Theology* (Kansas City: Sheed & Ward).
Mananzan, M.J.
 1995 'Feminist Theology in Asia: A Ten Years' Overview', *FemTh* 10: 21-32.
Mananzan, M., *et al.* (eds.)
 1996 *Women Resisting Violence: Spirituality for Life* (Maryknoll, NY: Orbis Books).
Marchbank, J. and G. Letherby
 2002 'Offensive and Defensive: Student Support and Higher Education Evaluation', in Howie and Tauchert (eds.).
Martin, F.
 1994 *The Feminist Question: Feminist Theology in the Light of Christian Tradition* (Edinburgh: T. & T. Clark).
May, M.
 1995 *A Body Knows: A Theopoetics of Death and Resurrection* (New York: Continuum).
Maynard, M.
 1993 'Violence Towards Women', in D. Richardson and V. Robinson (eds.), *Introducing Women's Studies* (London: Macmillan): 99-122.
McFadyen, A.
 2000 *Bound to Sin: Abuse, Holocaust and the Christian Doctrine of Sin* (Cambridge: Cambridge University Press).
McKay, H.A.
 1997 'On the Future of Feminist Biblical Criticism', in Brenner and Fontaine 1997: 61-83.
Methodist Conference in Britain
 1995 *A Cry of the Beloved.*
Mercadante, L.
 1990 *Gender, Doctrine and God: The Shakers and Contemporary Theology* (Nashville: Abingdon Press).
Miller-McLemore, B.J.
 1994 *Also a Mother: Work and Family as a Theological Dilemma* (Nashville: Abingdon Press).
 1996 'The Living Human Web: Pastoral Theology at the Turn of the Century', in Moessner 1996: 9-26.
 1998 'The Subject and Practice of Pastoral Theology as a Practical Theological Discipline: Pushing Past the Nagging Identity Crisis to the Poetics of Resistance', in Ackermann and Bons Storm: 175-98.
 1999 'Feminist Theory in Pastoral Theology', in Miller-McLemore and Gill-Austern 1999: 77-94.
Miller-McLemore, B.J. and B. Gill-Austern (eds.)
 1999 *Feminist and Womanist Pastoral Theology* (Nashville: Abingdon Press).
Milne, P.J.
 1997 'Towards Feminist Companionship', in Brenner and Fontaine 1997: 39-60.

Minear, P.S.
 1961 *Images of the Church in the New Testament* (London).
Moessner, J.S. (ed.)
 1996 *Through the Eyes of Women: Insights for Pastoral Care* (Minneapolis: Augsburg–Fortress).
Mollenkott, V.
 1986 *The Divine Feminine: The Biblical Imagery of God as Female* (New York: Crossroad).
Moltmann, J.
 1974 *The Crucified God: The Cross of Christ as the Foundation and Criticism of Christian Theology* (London: SCM Press).
Morley, J.
 1992 *All Desires Known* (London: SPCK).
Morton, S.A.
 1999 'To Suffer in Silence', *Inside Out: Journal of the Council for World Mission* 12: 6-9.
Mosala, I.J.
 1989 *Biblical Hermeneutics and Black Theology in South Africa* (Grand Rapids: Eerdmans).
Mudge, L.
 1999 'Human Solidarity in a Global Civilisation', in Ballard and Couture 1999: 27-31.
Namalambo, C.
 2001 *The Place of Catholic Women's Church Organisations in the Catholic Church in Zambia: A Study in Identity, Authority, Inculturation and Relationships* (MA thesis, School of Arts and Letters, Anglia Polytechnic University).
Neuger, C.C. (ed.)
 1996 *The Arts of Ministry: Feminist-Womanist Approaches* (Louisville, KY: Westminster/John Knox Press).
 2001 *Counseling Women: A Narrative, Pastoral Approach* (Philadelphia: Fortress Press).
Neuger, C.C., and J. Poling (eds.)
 1997 *The Care of Men* (Nashville: Abingdon Press).
Newsom, C.A., and S.H. Ringe (eds.)
 1992 *The Women's Bible Commentary* (London: SPCK).
Nouwen, H.J.M.
 1990 *The Wounded Healer: Ministry in Contemporary Society* (New York: Image Books [1972]).
Nussbaum, M.
 1986 *The Fragility of Goodness: Luck and Ethics in Greek Tragedy and Philosophy* (Cambridge: Cambridge University Press).
O'Faolain, J., and L. Martines (eds.)
 1979 *Not in God's Image: Women in History* (London: Virago).
Oden, T.
 1984 *Care of Souls in the Classic Tradition* (Philadelphia: Fortress Press).
Oduyoye, M.A.
 2001a *Introducing African Women's Theology* (IFT, 6; Sheffield: Sheffield Academic Press).

    2001b   'A Biblical Perspective on the Church', *Ecumenical Review* 53: 44-47.

Okure, T.

    1993   'Feminist Interpretations in Africa', in Schüssler Fiorenza 1993b: 76-85.

Ortner, S.B.

    1995   'Is Female to Male as Nature is to Culture?', in MacKinnon and McIntyre: 36-55.

Parsons S.F.

    2000   'Accounting for Hope: Feminist Theology as Fundamental Theology', in *Challenging Women's Orthodoxies in the Context of Faith* (Aldershot: Ashgate): 1-20.

Parsons, S.F. (ed.)

    2000   *Challenging Women's Orthodoxies in the Context of Faith* (Aldershot: Ashgate).

Pattison, S.

    2000   *Shame: Theory, Therapy, Theology* (Cambridge: Cambridge University Press).

Patton, J.

    1993   *Pastoral Care in Context: An Introduction to Pastoral Care* (Louisville, KY: Westminster/John Knox Press).

Pellauer, M.D.

    1985   'Moral Callousness and Moral Sensitivity: Violence Against Women', in B.H. Andolsen, C. Gudorf and M.D. Pellauer (eds.), *Women's Consciousness, Women's Conscience: A Reader in Feminist Ethics* (San Francisco: Harper & Row): 33-50.

Plaskow, J.

    1993   'Anti-Judaism in Feminist Christian Interpretation', in Schüssler Fiorenza 1993b: 117-29.

Procter-Smith, M.

    1990   *In Her Own Rite: Constructing Feminist Liturgical Tradition* (Nashville: Abingdon Press).

    1993   'Feminist Interpretation and Liturgical Proclamation', in Schüssler Fiorenza 1993b: 313-25.

    1995a   *Praying with our Eyes Open: Engendering Feminist Liturgical Prayer* (Nashville: Abingdon Press).

    1995b   'The Whole Loaf: Holy Communion and Survival', in Adams and Fortune 1995: 489-503.

Pryce, M.

    1996   *Finding a Voice: Men, Women and the Community of the Church* (London: SCM Press).

Ramsay, K.

    2000   'Losing One's Life for Others: Self-sacrifice Revisited', in Parsons 2000b: 121-33.

Ramshaw, G.

    1995   *God Beyond Gender: Feminist Christian God-language* (Philadelphia: Fortress Press).

Regnier-Bohler, D.

    1992   'Literary and Mystical Voices', in Klapisch-Zuber: 427-82.

Roberts, A., and J. Donaldson (eds.)

    1867   *The Writings of Clement of Alexandria* (Ante-Nicene Library, 4; Edinburgh: T. & T. Clark).

Ross, M.
    1988   *Pillars of Flame: Power, Priesthood and Spiritual Maturity* (London: SCM
                Press).
Ruether, R.R.
    1974   'Virginal Feminism in the Fathers of the Church', in R.R. Ruether (ed.),
                Religion and Sexism: Images of Women in the Jewish and Christian Traditions
                (New York: Simon & Schuster): 150-83.
    1975   *New Woman, New Earth: Sexist Ideologies and Human Liberation* (New York:
                Seabury).
    1981   *To Change the World: Christology and Cultural Criticism* (New York: Cross-
                road).
    1983   *Sexism and God-Talk: Toward a Feminist Theology* (London: SCM Press).
    1985a   *Womanguides: Readings towards a Feminist Theology* (Boston: Beacon Press).
    1985b   *Women-church: Theology and Practice of Feminist Liturgical Communities* (San
                Francisco: Harper & Row).
    1985c   'Feminist Interpretation: A Method of Correlation', in Russell 1985: 111-24.
    1989   *Disputed Questions: On Being a Christian* (Maryknoll, NY: Orbis Books).
    1991   'Christian Tradition and Feminist Hermeneutics', in Børresen 1991:
                267-91.
    1995   'Ecofeminism and Healing Ourselves, Healing the Earth', *FemTh* 9: 51-62.
    1996   'Ecofeminism: First and Third World Women', in Mananzan *et al.*: 27-35.
    1998   *Introducing Redemption in Christian Feminism* (IFT, 1; Sheffield: Sheffield
                Academic Press).
Russell, L.M.
    1985   *Feminist Interpretation of the Bible* (Philadelphia: Westminster Press).
    1993   *Church in the Round: Feminist Interpretation of the Church* (Louisville, KY:
                Westminster/John Knox Press).
    2001   'Hot-House Ecclesiology: A Feminist Interpretation of the Church',
                Ecumenical Review 53: 48-56.
Russell, L.M., and J.S. Clarkson (eds.)
    1996   *Dictionary of Feminist Theologies* (London: Mowbray).
Rutter, P.
    1989   *Sex in the Forbidden Zone: When Men in Power—Therapists, Doctors, Clergy,
                Teachers and Others—Betray Women's Trust* (London: Mandala).
Saiving, V.
    1995   'The Human Situation: A Feminine View' (1960), in MacKinnon and
                McIntyre 1995: 3-18.
Schüssler Fiorenza, E.
    1983   *In Memory of Her: A Feminist Theological Reconstruction of Christian Origins*
                (New York: Crossroad).
    1984   *Bread Not Stone: The Challenge of Feminist Biblical Interpretation* (Boston:
                Beacon Press).
    1990   'Missionaries, Apostles, Co-workers: Romans 16 and the Re-construction
                of Early Women's Christian History', in Loades 1990: 57-71.
    1992   *But She Said: Feminist Practices of Biblical Interpretation* (Boston: Beacon Press).
    1993a   *Discipleship of Equals: A Critical Feminist Ekklesia-logy of Liberation* (London:
                SCM Press).
    1998   *Sharing Her Word: Feminist Biblical Interpretation in Context* (Edinburgh: T. &
                T. Clark).

Schüssler Fiorenza, E. (ed.)
    1993b   *Searching the Scriptures: A Feminist Introduction* (London: SCM Press).
    1994   *Searching the Scriptures: A Feminist Commentary* (London: SCM Press).
Slee, N.
    2001   'Apophatic Faithing in Women's Spirituality', *BJTE* 11.2: 23-37.
Soskice, J.M.
    1987   *Metaphor and Religious Language* (Oxford: Clarendon Press).
    1992a   'Women's Problems', *Priests and People* 6: 301-306.
    1992b   'Can a Feminist call God "Father"?' in Elwes 1992: 15-30.
    1993   'The Truth Looks Different from Here', in H. Regan and A. Torrance (eds.), *Christ and Context: The Confrontation between Gospel and Culture* (Edinburgh: T. & T. Clark): 43-59.
    1996   'Turning the Symbols', in D. Hampson (ed.), *Swallowing a Fishbone? Feminist Theologians Debate Christianity* (London: SPCK): 17-32.
Stanley, L., and S. Wise
    1993   *Breaking Out Again: Feminist Ontology and Epistemology* (London: Routledge).
Stanton, E.C.
    1993 [1885]   *The Woman's Bible* (Boston: North Eastern University Press).
Storkey, E.
    2000   *Created or Constructed? The Great Gender Debate* (Carlisle: Paternoster Press).
Tamez, E.
    1988   'Women's Rereading of the Bible', in V. Fabella and M.A. Oduyoye (eds.), *With Passion and Compassion* (Maryknoll, NY: Orbis Books): 173-80.
    2001   'An Ecclesial Community: Women's Visions and Voices', *Ecumenical Review* 53: 57-63.
Tanner, M.
    2001   'Some Thoughts Inspired by the Ecumenical Community', *Ecumenical Review* 53: 64-71.
Thatcher, A.
    1999   *Marriage after Modernity: Christian Marriage in Postmodern Times* (STS, 3; Sheffield: Sheffield Academic Press).
Thistlethwaite, S.B.
    1990   *Sex, Race and God* (London: Geoffrey Chapman).
    1996   'Militarism in North American Perspective', in Mananzen *et al.* 1996: 119-25.
Thorne, H.
    2000   *Journey to Priesthood: An In-depth Study of the First Women Priests in the Church of England* (Bristol: Centre for Comparative Sudies in Religion and Gender, Department of Theology and Religious Studies, University of Bristol).
Tidball, D.
    1986   *Skilful Shepherds: An Introduction to Pastoral Theology* (Leicester: Inter-Varsity Press).
Trible, P.
    1984   *Texts of Terror* (Philadelphia: Fortress Press).
UNICEF
    1996   *State of the World's Children*.
Vanstone, W.H.
    1977   *Love's Endeavour, Love's Expense: The Response of Being to the Love of God* (London: Darton, Longman & Todd).

Walker Bynum, C.
    1982   *Jesus as Mother: Studies in the Spirituality of the High Middle Ages* (London:
                University of California Press).
Walton, H.
    1998   'Passion and Pain: Conceiving Theology out of Infertility', *Contact* 130: 3-9.
Watkins Ali, C.
                'A Womanist Search for Sources', in Miller-McLemore and Gill-Austern
                1999: 51-64.
WCC
    1982   *Baptism, Eucharist and Ministry* (Faith and Order Paper, n. 111; Geneva:
                WCC Publications).
    1997   *Living Letters: A Report of Visits to the Churches during the Ecumenical Decade—
                Churches in Solidarity with Women* (Geneva: WCC Publications).
    1990a   *Baptism, Eucharist and Ministry 1982–1990: Report on the Process and Responses*
                (Faith and Order Paper, n. 149; Geneva: WCC).
    1990b   *Church and World: The Unity of the Church and the Renewal of Human
                Community: A Faith and Order Study Document* (Faith and Order Paper, n.
                151; Geneva: WCC).
    2000   'On Being Church: Women's Voices and Visions', *Ecumenical Review* 53.1.
Webster, A.
    1995   *Found Wanting: Women, Christianity and Sexuality* (London: Cassell, Petter,
                Galpin & Co.).
West, A.
    1995   *Deadly Innocence: Feminism and the Mythology of Sin* (London: Cassell, Petter,
                Galpin & Co.).
Westcott House
    1991   ACCM 22 submission.
Williams, J.
    1992   'The Doctrine of the Trinity: A Way Forward for Feminists?', in Elwes
                1992: 31-43.
Winter, M.T.
    1991   *Woman Wisdom: A Feminist Lectionary and Psalter* (North Blackburn, Victoria:
                Collins Dove).
    1997   *Woman Prayer Woman Song: Resources for Ritual* (New York: Crossroad).
Woodward, J., and S. Pattison (eds.)
    2000   *The Blackwell Reader in Pastoral and Practical Theology* (Oxford: Basil Black-
                well).
Woolway, J.
    1997   'Edmund Spenser and the Culture of Place' (unpublished DPhil thesis,
                Oxford: Oxford University Press).
Wootton, J.
    2000   *Introducing a Practical Feminist Theology of Worship* (IFT, 5; Sheffield: Shef-
                field Academic Press).
Yee, G.A.
    1992   'Hosea', in Newsom and Ringe 1992: 195-202.
Zizioulas, J.
    1985   *Being as Communion: Studies in Personhood and the Church* (New York: St
                Vladimir's Seminary Press).

INDEXES

INDEX OF REFERENCES

BIBLE

Other books in the
Introductions in Feminist Theology series

Introducing African Women's Theology
Mercy Amba Oduyoye

Mercy Amba Oduyoye describes the context and methodology of Christian theology by Africans in the past two decades, offering brief descriptions and sample treatments of theological issues such as creation, Christology, ecclesiology, and eschatology. The daily spiritual life of African Christian women is evident as the reader is led to the sources of African women's Christian theology. This book reflects how African culture and its multi-religious context has influenced women's selection of theological issues.
ISBN 1-84127-143-8
Paper, 136 pages
£12.95

Introducing Asian Feminist Theology
Kwok Pui-Lan

The book introduces the history, critical issues, and direction of feminist theology as a grass roots movement in Asia. Kwok Pui-Lan takes care to highlight the diversity of this broad movement, noting that not all women theologians in Asia embrace feminism. Amid a diverse range of sociopolitical, religiocultural, postcultural, and postcolonial contexts, this book lifts up the diversity of voices and ways of doing feminist theology while attending to women's experiences, how the Bible is interpreted, and the ways that Asian religious traditions are appropriated. It searches out a passionate, life-affirming spirituality through feminine images of God, new metaphors for Christ, and a reformulation of sin and redemption.
ISBN 1-84127-066-0
Paper, 136 pages
£12.95

Introducing Body Theology
Lisa Isherwood and Elizabeth Stuart

Because Christianity asserts that God was incarnated in human form, one might expect that its theologies would be body affirming. Yet for women (and indeed also for gay men) the body has been the site for oppression. *Introducing Body Theology* offers a body-centered theology that discusses cosmology, ecology, ethics, immortality, and sexuality, in a concise introduction that proposes and encourages a positive theology of the body.
ISBN 1-85075-995-2
Paper, 168 pages
£12.95

Introducing Feminist Images of God
Mary Grey

Mary Grey presents recent thinking reflecting early attempts to move beyond restrictive God language, opening up the possibilities of more inclusive ways of praying. The rich experiences of God, distinctive and diverse, are seen through the eyes of many different cultures and the women who struggle for justice. Using the figure of Sophia Wisdom as an example, Grey shows that there are many still-unplumbed images of God to discover.
ISBN 1-84127-160-8
Paper, 136 pages
£12.95

Introducing a Practical Feminist Theology of Worship
Janet Wootton

Only three great women-songs are retained in the Bible: Deborah's song for ordinary people, Hannah's song of triumph, and Mary's song at meeting her cousin Elizabeth. Many others, such as Miriam's song, are truncated or over-shadowed by male triumphs. *Introducing a Practical Feminist Theology of Worship* begins by revealing how women have been 'whispering liturgy.' It then explores female images of God, discusses how worship spaces function, and

offers practical suggestions for how women can use words and movements to construct authentic forms of worship.
ISBN 1-84127-067-9
Paper, 148 pages
£12.95

Introducing Redemption in Christian Feminism
Rosemary R. Ruether

Introducing Redemption in Christian Feminism explores the dichotomy between two patterns of thinking found in Christianity: the redemption of Christ being applied to all without regard to gender, and the exclusion of women from leadership because women were created subordinate to men and because women were more culpable for sin. After examining these two patterns, Ruether examines some key theological themes: Christology, the self, the cross, and eschatology.
ISBN 1-85075-888-3
Paper, 136 pages
£12.95

Introducing Thealogy: Discourse on the Goddess
Melissa Raphael

Introducing Thealogy provides an accessible but critical introduction to the relationship of religion, theo/alogy, and gender, especially as these concepts unfold in the revival of Goddess religion among feminists in Europe, North America, and Australasia. Raphael focuses on the boundaries of that broad movement, what is meant by the Goddess, theology in history and ethics, the political implications of the movement, and how it relates to feminist witchcraft.
ISBN 1-85075-975-8
Paper, 184 pages
£12.95

Introducing Feminist Christologies
Lisa Isherwood

In this imaginative book, Lisa Isherwood challenges the oppressive model of an all-powerful God and highlights feminist interpretations of Christ across the globe. She attempts to chart a course from questioning the relevance of a male savior to women—to the many faces of Christ that have emerged from the lives of women (Jesus as lover, friend, or shaman, amongst other things)—to a place of reflection about the nature of Christological thinking in the twenty-first century.
ISBN 1-84127-250-7
Paper, 144 pages
£14.99

FEMINIST THEOLOGY TITLES

Individual Titles in Feminist Theology

Linda Hogan, *From Women's Experience to Feminist Theology*

Lisa Isherwood and Dorothea McEwan (eds.), *An A–Z of Feminist Theology*

Lisa Isherwood and Dorothea McEwan, *Introducing Feminist Theology*

Kathleen O'Grady, Ann L. Gilroy and Janette Patricia Gray (eds.), *Bodies, Lives, Voices: Gender in Theology*

Melissa Raphael, *Thealogy and Embodiment: The Post-Patriarchal Reconstruction of Female Sacrality*

Deborah Sawyer and Diane Collier (eds.), *Is There a Future for Feminist Theology?*

Lisa Isherwood (ed.), *The Good News of the Body: Sexual Theology and Feminism*

Alf Hiltebeitel and Kathleen M. Erndl, *Is the Goddess a Feminist? The Politics of South Asian Goddesses*

Introductions in Feminist Theology

Rosemary Ruether, *Introducing Redemption in Christian Feminism*

Lisa Isherwood and Elizabeth Stuart, *Introducing Body Theology*

Melissa Raphael, *Introducing Thealogy: Discourse on the Goddess*

Pui-lan Kwok, *Introducing Asian Feminist Theology*

Janet H. Wootton, *Introducing a Practical Feminist Theology of Worship*

Mary Grey, *Introducing Feminist Images of God*

Mercy Amba Oduyoye, *Introducing African Women's Theology*

Lisa Isherwood, *Introducing Feminist Christologies*

Feminist Companion to the Bible (1st Series)

Athalya Brenner (ed.), *A Feminist Companion to the Song of Songs*

Athalya Brenner (ed.), *A Feminist Companion to Genesis*

Athalya Brenner (ed.), *A Feminist Companion to Ruth*

Athalya Brenner (ed.), *A Feminist Companion to Judges*

Athalya Brenner (ed.), *A Feminist Companion to Samuel–Kings*

Athalya Brenner (ed.), *A Feminist Companion to Exodus–Deuteronomy*

Athalya Brenner (ed.), *A Feminist Companion to Esther, Judith and Susanna*

Athalya Brenner (ed.), *A Feminist Companion to the Latter Prophets*

Athalya Brenner (ed.), *A Feminist Companion to the Wisdom Literature*

Athalya Brenner (ed.), *A Feminist Companion to the Hebrew Bible in the New Testament*

Athalya Brenner and Carole Fontaine (eds.), *A Feminist Companion to Reading the Bible: Approaches, Methods and Strategies*

Feminist Companion to the Bible (2nd Series)

Athalya Brenner and Carole Fontaine (eds.), *Wisdom and Psalms*

Athalya Brenner (ed.), *Genesis*

Athalya Brenner (ed.), *Judges*

Athalya Brenner (ed.), *Ruth and Esther*

Athalya Brenner (ed.), *Samuel and Kings*

Athalya Brenner (ed.), *Exodus–Deuteronomy*

Athalya Brenner (ed.), *Prophets and Daniel*